The Corridor of Life

PIUS YAO ASHIARA

Archway Publishing books may be ordered through booksellers or by contacting:

Archway Publishing
1663 Liberty Drive
Bloomington, IN 47403
www.archwaypublishing.com
1-(888)-242-5904

Because of the dynamic nature of the Internet, any web addresses or links contained in this book may have changed since publication and may no longer be valid. The views expressed in this work are solely those of the author and do not necessarily reflect the views of the publisher, and the publisher hereby disclaims any responsibility for them.

Any people depicted in stock imagery provided by Thinkstock are models, and such images are being used for illustrative purposes only.

Certain stock imagery © Thinkstock.

ISBN: 978-1-4808-0701-3 (sc)
ISBN: 978-1-4808-0702-0 (hc)
ISBN: 978-1-4808-0703-7 (e)

Printed in the United States of America

Archway Publishing rev. date: 04/25/2014

CONTENTS

DEDICATION

This work is dedicated to the Almighty Everlasting God, who has given all life and this earth to live on. We acknowledge His greatness with gratitude.

To the Late Honorable Senator Frank Lautenberg

A great man who shared the aches, pains, and suffering of his fellow men and women and helped solve their problems. We acknowledge his love, kindness, and leadership. Let us give him a big applause and may he rest in perfect peace.

To My Late Parents:

Mr. Augustine K. Ashiara and Mrs. Salome Ashiara,
who always had hope in their children and prayed for them.

To My Wife:

Dansowah Ama Ashiara — A great wife and a wonderful mother. May our love last forever.

To My Children:

Victor Kwame Ashiara
Kevin Agbeko Ashiara
Christine Sena Ashiara
Dorothy Aku Ashiara
[I cannot thank you all enough for your support in my undertakings. You have been the stove under me that kept me boiling. Ours is a true relationship of father, sons, and daughters, friends, advisors, and companion. It is remarkable indeed.]

To Clark and Janet Faulkner:

The copy editing was done by Mrs. Janet Faulkner alone under extreme difficulties. She is a formidable wife, mother, a hard worker, and with the husband, a rare great married couple one will hardly ever find. Her husband, Mr. Clark Faulkner, and children, Andrea Christine Faulkner and Bruce Wesley Faulkner were very supportive of our projects. They are the best family friends to have. May God bless them!

INTRODUCTION

The Corridor of Life

Life comes to everyone in a second, and it is spent in a second, but only once. It comes with unknown prescribed amount of time and withdrawn on own time in a second – then our cry follows.

—Pius Yao Ashiara

Life is a baby to feed to grow.

—Pius Yao Ashiara

"The Corridor of Life" is Life's Guidance: From birth to death. Life is a journey that you will be traveling with hope of reaching the final destination of your life. The instruction is to take it with *only* joy and happiness. "The Corridor of Life," is book that will help the reader make a meaning and understanding of life.

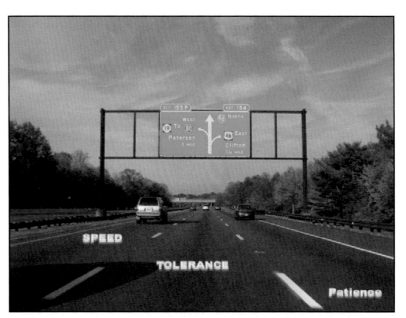

Figure 1: This is the highway of life with divided Lanes of Speed; Tolerance and Patience.

You are born into a world with many other people of several races — the white race, the black race, the African-American, Asian, Caucasian, etc. Know that everyone is to live in the world without being pushed around by another or pushed out. Life is birth here, passing away there, birth there, passing away here.

Birth: Before we begin to live we must visit the cemetery to observe tombstones of the dead, which give us an idea of the duration of time we might live. The epitaphs on these tombstones read: "He was born in 16... (Sixteen Hundred) and he died in 17... (Seventeen hundred). Here is an advice given to us that we will not be living forever and we must live our lives carefully, one day at a time, to get the most out of it, and before leaving this earth, we must leave some accomplished work for posterity.

Man: God made the world and put man in charge of the Garden of Eden (our earth). In loneliness He gave him a companion, a woman, by using one of his ribs to form her. There the unity of mankind began.

Woman: Woman was glad she came into a man's life to be a companion. In their union they violated the laws of God given to them in the Garden of Eden not to eat a fruit tree, and this became a curse on mankind. This influence became a temptation in man.

Marriage: The courtship between a man and a woman develops into marriage, bringing children into the world, and then the world begins to multiply.

Father: Man and woman were made to procreate and multiply the children of the earth. Sex was meant to multiply children and was not to use for pleasure.

Mother: Through multiplication woman became a mother with sons and daughters. Thus a man and woman became father and mother who built a home for the family.

Children: When children come into this world brought out by a mother and a father, they have an obligation to the children, promising the fulfillment of God's order that they will raise them as good human beings with love for them.

Mind: God fashioned man and woman with a brain from which the mind develops. The mind is to rule the earth in which we live and that is to govern all our lives and its activities.

Reverence for the Almighty Dollar: The Almighty Dollar is god that passes through every hand and through every transaction. **"IN GOD WE TRUST"** is the spirit of the dollar that is abused through drugs, murder, sex, counterfeits, greed, etc., which is blasphemy to God. A new life and spirit is put back into the dollar now. *Long illness or death will come to those who adulterate, disrespect, and abuse it in any other way other than through work and thinking.*

The Perception of Life and America: Everything to live by is provided by God through thinking. Problems, difficulties, tragedies, sorrows, accidents, and death will come to us in our travels, and we must learn to bear them with courage and fortitude. "God Bless America" should be the prayer at everyone's lips.

Chapter 1

TAKING THE TRIP WITH MANHOOD OR WOMANHOOD

Life is like a car. Once we are out of the womb, we are to catch an entrance and enter the highway of life by taking a lane with speed, but we must be watching, with caution, for road signs. Some places will have cones. Some will have speed signs posted with 25 mph, 30 mph, 35 mph, 40 mph, 45 mph, 50 mph, 55 mph and 65 mph. Although the car is built to run 200 miles or more an hour, we still have to drive it with caution, observing nature, to reach old age. Any speed over these posted signs will attract punishment, i.e., fines or jail sentences, and so it is with life as well. We could develop sickness through overexertion and abuse.

Life is a construction road that is never finished leading forward, and you build it as you go along. When a road is being constructed through a land (through life), it meets difficulties. The bushes and trees must be cleared, then the ground has to be dug and boulders and rocks removed. *Your life has to be designed like clothes to fit you. Your taste, style, and looks will then blend in.*

Figure 1: Life as a car.

One thing that will benefit a new traveler who is planning a trip to an unknown country will be to go on fact-finding mission to understand the facts and culture of the place and how to prepare.

Man! First, before you begin your journey through this life, you must identify yourself as a superior creature – demigod. *A man with power to direct his own affairs at all cost, and he is superior to all creatures on earth and inanimate objects.*

Here comes the preparation. A man must draw a map for himself to follow. His map must contain some divine virtues that he strictly adheres to. He must draw rules and principles against littleness and low life. He must constantly pound his head for the best to be brought out and always thinking ahead and looking ahead, but working hard and looking forward for the best results.

Political Leadership: A man swears upon the Bible and promises his people he will be a mayor, governor, senator, or the President. The next thing he finds is that a charge is brought against him by the people who elected him into the position by taking what I will call "minimum wage-earner coffee money" – $3,000, $7,000, $10,000 bribe?

The place a politician occupies is a coveted position, and many members in society will find ways and means to shake the ladder so that he falls. Great heights are where all eyes are turned to see what is happening there. Immediately when a man is elected into a position of power, he must realize that all eyes are going to focus on him, because what he is in charge of belongs to them, and they are going to ask for accountability. He has accepted the responsibility, and of course, there must be accountability.

A man must turn himself into a car on sale at the dealership and place a "Quality Control" sticker on himself to see how much anyone will pay to be "completely satisfied." After he determines his "Quality Control," then he can move forward and make his choices in life – education, employment, marriage, etc.

If he wants to educate himself, first he must do three things:

1. Learn to hide into himself and be an avid reader of all kinds of works produced by great men and women;
2. Turn himself into a sponge and absorb knowledge and ideas from all sources;
3. Turn his back to the crowd until the goal is realized.

Challenges a man faces in life: Once a man is born into this world, he faces challenges. He cannot settle for less for his life. Any move made to bring a change is a challenge. If he plants a seed, he faces a challenge for keeping it grow. It is good a man takes something worthy in his hands to grow with it. Many times life has to beat on him to mold him.

There are three types of effort makers:

1. Few will jump into the water without direction and start swimming;
2. Some will study the movement of the sea before making any effort;
3. The majority will wait to see others swim before making an attempt.

[This is what I will call self-reliance or self-dependence] Everyman is born to grow on his own. Before he can do this, he must study trees and see how they form and how they grow. Every tree grows independently, but takes its strength from the soil seeking its food from rain, sun, and the wind. What about animals in the bush? They live on their own but take their living from nature. Trees face challenges too. Vicious weeds intersperse with some of them. Some surround them and try to suffocate or impede their progress and growth. But many assert their own singleness of purpose and thrive through their difficult encounters. A man cannot grow off another man. He cannot be a tree grown off another tree. He needs to reach the soil on his own to develop his own roots – that way he is firmer. We see trees weather-beaten; their leaves fall during winter time. That is how they cry. Naked before the cold and snow, they have no one to help them, but they maintain their inner strength and fight.

Labeling yourself: Stop labeling yourself, "I am an old fool. What do I know?" "I am a black man." "I am a white man." "I am a punk." "I am a no-good-for-nothing man." "I am a lost man; I am a hopeless man. I can't be a good husband or can't be a good mother." You are a person with dignity; appreciate it. You can always be good if you want to be good, because goodness is inside you and not outside of you. Everything that makes a car run is inside that car and not outside of it, and everything that makes a person create, build, or do anything or move is inside of him or her – power, spirit, and soul are there.

The graveyard is the only thing that is never satisfied and is always asking for more. The more it takes hold of a man, the less interested a man is in other human beings and essential things in life, even perhaps God.

We grow from babies into boys (youth). We then develop into men. A true man becomes a husband, and when he does well in that capacity, he becomes a father with more responsibilities — with accountability waiting for him in old age. And ultimately he becomes a grandfather, at the last stage giving attention to his grandchildren.

The human being is the universe wrapped into a small package.

—*Pius Yao Ashiara*

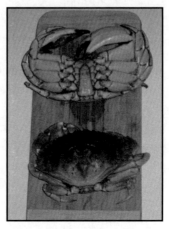

Figure 2. Fish and Crab are divided into two parts as shown in this picture.

Every human being is divided into two parts by the spinal cord. And so are all animals and the fishes of the sea. The two parts are *left* and *right*. The left is the *gentle* part; the right is the *tough* or hard part. The *left* part is less used by most people, but the *right* part is constantly in use by many people – the animal side. We have the capacity to make ourselves superior beings without help from other animals.

On human side (Left): (Gentle): One side is *humane,* and the other side is *animal*. On the human side, we pray and worship God. We marry. We speak. We sing. We laugh. We are kind and compassionate. We train our minds into reasoning human beings. We build homes. We love and care about each other. We boil water or cook food before we eat. We think. We wear clothes and shoes on our bodies. We read and write. We go to school. We develop the mind and build skills and machinery – bicycles, motorcycles, cars, trains, airplanes and ships and so on. We train ourselves into medical doctors and are able to treat our own medical problems. We are able to perform medical surgery and bring healing to ourselves. Whatever animals do, they cannot do like us. Though they are also animals, they are without the capacity to function as man and woman. They live and do things by instinct. Animals cannot do what we do.

On Animal side (Right) (Tough): On the animal side, we are rough. We eat raw fruits. We show aggression. We are luscious. We are wicked, bad, and evil. We run and jump like animals. We fear things. We show anger, hate, envy, jealousy, and greed, and we are revengeful. We fight each other. We are wild. We dance. We are impatient and play sports with aggressiveness like animals. We are unreasonable at times (these are animal behaviors). We kill. Anything violent or which entails force comes from our animal side.

> *Youth is the seed, but old age is the crop.*
>
> —*Pius Yao Ashiara*

We have three worlds of learning. In youth it is best for us to choose one category in which to stay:

1. **A scholar** went to school all his life and received several certificates, diplomas, or degrees. He went to work relying on his paper qualification and is showy on his paper qualification;
2. **An educated person** is a person who produces something with his years of learning for others to think about or work on further;
3. **A thinker** is a person who doesn't concern himself too much about academics or classroom education but takes one area of human need and spends his lifetime bringing out great results. Examples are Thomas Edison, Henry Ford, Steve Jobs, Bill Gates, etc.

> *Man/woman is the power of God on earth.*
>
> —*Pius Yao Ashiara*

Man and woman are the power of God on earth. They are supreme over all things on earth: Animals, the sea, lakes, rivers, sky, the mountains, the trees, boulders, stones, rocks – everything. But then, every other living thing on earth is a *"small man or woman."*

Man in his supremacy and power reached into the forest and said to the tiger, "You are *small man. I am your master. Follow me!*

"I built you a zoo where I can study you." Man reached to the sea, rivers, sky, mountains, and the trees and said, "You are the sea, you are a *small man.*

"I built a ship to travel over you. I put you on a screen saver of the computer to teach grandeur." Looking into the sky, he said, "Sky! You are a *small man.*

"I built an aircraft to fly over you. I put you on a screen saver of the computer to teach me vision." Man stood before the mountain and said "You are a *small man.*

"You cannot frighten me with your size. Stand afar and I will climb atop of you. To show my power over the earth, I put you on a screen saver of the computer to teach me magnificence and altitude."

Man is an eagle over all birds in the sky. He is the greatest of all birds. His power and ingenuity made a "metal bird" in the air. When a man walks by a strange dog and it barks at him, the owner shouts at it and says, "Stop it!" The dog mellows; it calms down. It takes the order from his master: *man*. But man is bigger when he has vision. When we have eyes we ought to have vision.

Thomas Alva Edison, for an instance, built a laboratory around himself where he worked day and night, not allowing anyone to take up his time. He associated with few friends with similar goals.

Henry Ford was an ordinary mechanic; though he had no academic education, he developed himself into an extraordinary engineer with a goal. He listened inside of him and said, "I want to build cars, and that is what I will do and nothing else. Let the world laugh at me if I fail." And the result of his resolution and goal became Ford Motor Company, employing thousands of workers and giving food and mobility to people the world around.

Every man has in life a message written in his palms. If he looks into two or more palms of other men he will observe that the signs in each hand are different. Some men want to be like some else. John wants to be Michael, because Michael was a pop singer, though he doesn't have a voice to be a singer. How many boys or men never wanted to be Michael Jackson? But when Michael Jackson passed away, how many boys or men asked to die with him? Since no one dies alongside another, it tells us to be our own person. Unless a man is able to identify himself as a man, he will be making a mockery of himself in the eyes of God.

A dog is an animal and is a dog. A lion is an animal and is a lion. A tiger is an animal and is a tiger. They don't change and cannot change from what they are made to be, but man tries to change. John wants to be Michael, because Michael is popular. Michael wants to change to John, because John is a good public speaker. Peter wants to be Paul. No animal changes. A fish is a fish. A blue fish is a blue fish. A porgy is a porgy. A goat is a goat. They are what they are and unique in their individual ways, and they ought to be what they are. Man is the biggest of all animals; that is why it is frivolous to change into somebody else. The chameleon is an animal that changes by the look of other things that appear before it, but this is a lesson it teaches us: Living human beings change in character and environment and taste only and not in their sexes and what they are as human beings.

DIFFERENT KIND OF MEN:

Some men were parking attendants yesterday, today they are grocery store owners, and tomorrow they are building contractors. Two years from now they envision building apartment complexes; some out of the blue became plumbers, and now suddenly they must become shipping agents – jack-of-all-trade.

Some men stay with a woman this year and have a baby. Next year you find them knocking on another woman's door, and what you know next is another baby and they disappear. And when you ask, "What happened to Alice and your son?" All he says is, "Alice is only good in bed; that is all you can get out of her. I don't waste time on such a woman," he would blurt out. He never talks about himself. It is always the other person with faults. He is always an angel before others.

Some men talk in large terms of what kind of properties they own. "I bought a 600-acre property near the ocean with cash. It has a fine deck and so on. They tell you, "My wife's birthday is next week, and I am going to the car dealership to buy her the latest Lexus. At first I thought of financing it, but I thought otherwise to buy it by cash, since I have the money" when he can't even afford a bicycle for himself.

When it comes to "table talk," the conversation comes to what kind of education they acquired "I was in Harvard Law School for a year, and my mother became ill, so I had to withdraw to take care of her" ¯ when they don't even know the campus.

Some men turn themselves into a balloon and are all over the place. They are in the air, being held in the hands by others, but still flying out, showing what color they are. Such "balloon type" of men lay flat on the ground when a little pin pokes them, and no one sees them anymore.

Some treat women as underwear, changing them as used — not even taking the time to wash them and think of them as something into which work was put by parents. And they like variety. They are not used to one woman and like to experiment with differences, but the same sexual organs.

Some in courtship or marriage turn a woman into a bird and pluck all her feathers so that she cannot fly away at will — not teaching or guiding her in anything so that he will always be the boss or master.

Some I call "catch-and-throw." They go with a woman awhile and let go. They use a woman like a paper towel to wipe the hands and then throw it into a waste basket. Then they move onto another one, making a baby or two then disappear.

Some I call "ladder holders." They hold the ladder for the other man to climb atop and be in charge of them. Every time they are asked to do something or take charge of a situation, they point to another person. "He does it better than me. Let him take the floor — he is good at it." *They never believe in themselves.*

Some turn their lives into scratching lottery tickets to be instant winners in life. Can you imagine how many tickets they must buy to be winners? The biggest winners are those who work with their hands and don't spend time scratching tickets. Many of these lottery ticket buyers are the poorest and uneducated. Instead of trusting the almighty words "IN GOD WE TRUST" by working, they take the easy way out. They walk to the counter and ask for number two, then scratch it but do not win. Then they ask for number three and scratch it and lose again. Then they turn to Pick-Six but wait for its result the next day when it played. (Before you buy a lottery ticket talk to Mr. Warren Buffet and Mr. Bill Gates and other rich people how safe is it to gamble).

Some are what I call "sleeping hogs": not willing to work but will find enough food to eat and not worry about what to expect next. They are just like Falstaff. They are happy where they stand in life and pleased with the status quo.

Some are what I call "makeshift pastors or preachers." Out of the blue, you find them wearing pastor clothes with the little white shirt protruding through the coat. They learn a few verses of the Bible and claim they are visionaries or prophets. They pretend to have magical powers to exorcise evil spirits from another person.

Some I call "bitter-lips." What comes out under their tongues is horrible — abusive and verbally insulting. One insults a partner and her family members. If there were any deficiencies or flaws he knew in that family, he will always bring it up in every argument. "Your father is a jerk. He robbed Bank of America, and everyone in your neighborhood knew it." He would blurt it out in an argument, insulting even a past life.

For some "I am the man or the boss. What I say is what holds." Any other approach or suggestion from his partner is never good enough.

Some men are time wasters. They think they have so much time and will waste others' time, too. No matter what happens, they are never on time.

Some are heavy drinkers and smokers. They will talk in large terms of brand names of liquor and how much they know about drinks and how heavily they can drink and smoke. Some have smoked so much that it turned the teeth black with a disgusting smell coming from their breath.

Some love money and like to have it constantly, like the human breath. They will go to any length to get it, regardless of the risk involved. If there were a money tree under the ocean and no torpedoes to go there, they would invent any scheme to reach it, instead of working and earning it.

Some are car lovers. The car is their demigod. They will keep it clean 24 hours a day. When they drive it outside, it must be parked far away from other vehicles. It must be garage kept and polished at all times to shine like the glittering sun.

Some men have what I call "side dish women." They use such women for recreation and pleasure only and, if they can, get money out of them as well.

Some are very neat outwardly and well dressed but don't care too much about mind development or take time in thinking and improvement of their personality, let alone have a decent profession or career. When asked, he has a story to tell. He has lately applied for a managerial position with the Chase Manhattan Bank would be the answer.

Some are liars and can lie to the teeth. They would keep a straight face without the slightest compunction and lie about a thing.

Some are women users. They like to get out of a woman 200 miles to a gallon, and they will do anything to get the maximum of what they put into her — food, clothes, or sex. If it is a ride, they make sure they get it somewhere off the woman.

Some men are like birds. They fly and perch on one tree then another. Before you know it, they fly away into the sky and disappear.

Some of these men go to bed with a woman because they are usually in a hurry to get work done; they take the underwear off by throwing it on the floor. As soon as they are finished with the sexual escapade, they go out and buy a pack of cigarettes and take half; they give the rest to the woman and probably would not see them again.

Some are loan sharks. They demand more interest on loans given out to friends or others and are more than shylock in "Merchant of Venice."

Some men turn their penis into a windshield wiper, propelling it from left to right as long as they maintain the sex desire.

Some men's mouth is filled with filth. They do not care about what comes out of their mouths and so disrespect everyone. Words from them fly like sheets of paper from an assembly line. Some, when they become angry or irritated, use their tongues with no reference to the rules of courtesy, propriety, or self-respect.

Some men are tow trucks. They prefer to be towed. Someone has to change the flat tire or jump-start them before they can function as true human beings.

Some men are neat freaks. They do not like dirt. They will not allow dirt or anything that is not clean to come close to them.

Some like to have a moustache or bear and comes around with a little pocket comb running through it.

Some like to grow hair on the chest and overgrow their armpit with hair which they turn into "lover's pet" during romance.

Some have taken drug dealing as their profession and are never deterred by law enforcement officers.

Some men do not study a woman before marrying her or going to bed with her and evidently sell their regrets to other men.

Some men talk and pride themselves about how good their wives are in handling the home.

Some men talk about what kind of position their wives hold in the office. When it comes to "table talk" about their wives and the conversation comes to what kind of education they have acquired, he would say, "She has a PhD in Psychology and she is the Dean of University of Hard-knock."

Some men are very greedy. When they head a company they must enjoy the most benefit not caring about the rank-and-file.

Some men do not respect women. This happens when a woman is in charge and they don't like her orders.

Some men who are very handsome and beautiful take advantage of their good look and "walk over" women in making choices. They see one and look her over thoroughly and say she is not good; the next one is not good enough, and the third one: "I don't like her. Her nails are too long."

Some men are very fast and "bang" on women here and there without thinking about how much they take from them.

Some men are finger pointers. "Let Mr. Johnson handle the situation. He knows how to handle such issues."

Some men are very gentle and weak in nature. They can't handle tough situations that confront them and would rather let his wife face up to it.

Some men are extremely slow and take forever to do anything, not worrying about an appointment. They will spend the whole time making choices between neckties.

For some men, sex is their catch. Once a woman would give it to him he has patience enough to wait on her.

Some men love material possessions. They will hoard everything until the garage has no place.

Some men are very neat but very dirty in character. They will explore every kind of woman on this earth, and they are never satisfied with what comes to them. If they are given a finger, they don't want a finger but a whole hand.

Some men go with a woman to find out if she is looking for an "overnight ride" or someone good to marry.

Some men love clothes. They will buy every kind and style on the market without regard for the cost.

Some do not respect women in authority or position and consider them subordinates not fit to be in charge of them;

Some cannot take pain and suffering. A little illness sends them screaming all over and calling their wives to their sick bed.

Some men are everywhere when they have a little authority. These I call "Mister-All-over." Authority consumes them in such a way as if they were ready to lift the world on their two hands.

Some men's love is beautiful and eternally filled with honey and a clean heart.

Some know that to reach a woman's heart is by the tongue and they will sweet talk them into an agreement.

Some men know we have to live by household chores, but some leave the tasks to their wives yet expect an orderly home.

Instinctively, a man would always like to hold his place as a man and the boss regardless of his worthiness — this is natural.

Many men have refused to learn to cook and will wait on the wife to come home to make dinner.

Some men are greedy and would want more of anything.

Some men, when they have the support of a woman, would never do anything to forward their own affairs. Thus, they remain permanently under a woman's influence and guidance.

Some men like to dish out money to their women or wives to keep them in one place.

Just like women, some men are charge it now, but worry about payment later.

Some men have made their wives windshield wipers so that they will be in control of the car.

Some men like to proclaim their marriage problems, aloud, so others know what is going in the relationship.

Some men are extremely jealous in love and can be very evil or spiteful if anyone intrudes on their relationship.

Some men prefer dating married women as opposed to dating single women. They consider those cleaner women.

When a man becomes a father, he turns to be more responsible than if he were single.

When a man becomes a father and a woman is absent, he comes into a bind not knowing what to do.

Some parents warn their sons against marrying a particular woman. If they did marry, she may not be satiated with her needs.

Some men are also "authority brokers." They like to order their women around and be in charge all the time.

Some men turn a relationship into a trailer or a dog so that a woman is a follower.

Some men fail to develop some good qualities of man that could aid them later in their personal lives. They just refuse to grow.

Some men put a twisted rope into a relationship so that a woman is tied into one spot and always begging for her needs.

Just like some women, some men are shoplifters. A visit to a friend's home finds something missing.

A man is a torchbearer or a guiding light for a woman. His duty is to see her grow.

Some men are nagging, and some are careless and irresponsible homeowners.

With a man choosing a woman for a relationship, he must determine two things about her. "Is she ambitious and is she a person with good conscience?" This must be his question.

A man may have a child or two with a woman in their early years of the relationship, where the woman failed completely to make the best of herself. But a wise man, because of his children, will try to train his woman so that she will be there to help raise the children. If a man focuses on her deficiency rather than training her, he will lose more than the woman; besides, her children will grow up without a mother, which will not be good for the children's future.

With some men, every time they form a friendship with a woman, the next thing they know she fades out of the picture and another chance is gone. With some men, when a woman goes with them, she stays for only a short period of time. They take another one, and she disappears. Why such things happen to them may be that something personal about them is repellant. In such a case, a man must study himself to find out what is wrong maybe a kind of perfume he uses or a body problem. A thorough personal investigation should help discover what is wrong.

A man turns to be bitter when some injustice is done to his woman or wife and he likes to retaliate.

Some men in a relationship with a woman turn it into a car and let his mother (mother-in-law of his woman) drive it her way — this is common in marriages.

When a man is sick in a relationship and seeking help from her woman he is more humble and respectful to her.

When a man is angry in a relationship the way he punishes her partner or spouse is he refuses to sleep with her.

A man's looks at times, rather than his character, holds a woman in one place. And the man who knows how to use his good charms wins her.

Some married men may have an outside relationship with another married woman where she becomes pregnant, then brings the child to her marriage without the husband knowing. This brings child of different character into a marriage. This is a wrong done by some married men in marriage.

Some men have "good teeth" and know how to get more out of a woman, turn her into a shish kebab on a pick, and pull the meat off one bite at a time until everything is finished off the pick and before a woman knows she is left a pick without meat and it is too late for her to realize it.

Some men really like sex and desire the strokes that keep them afloat with captivating joy and like to go as many times their energy can take them.

Some men use pyjamas or robe to provoke a woman into sex.

When a man has a woman or a wife, but he is interested in another woman, he talks down his wife to gain the acceptance of his new interest. "Oh, my wife does not sleep or cook for me anymore — she lost interest me that is what he will say of the wife."

Some men after they sleep with a woman, they turn her into a "joke" and prostitute and ask other men to partake. [If this is a married woman and the husband finds out, it could result in murder of the wrongdoer].

A man or a husband may note that people change in a relationship; love and woman can easily change to his astonishment.

Some men are, at times, in two places in a relationship. They make the top look good to hold a woman to them, but deep down in the heart, it is a ploy.

Some men "waste" women. Like apples, they bite each a bit and dump it back into the basket without completely eating them to a finish thus making them redundant.

Some married men coax another woman into a relationship by lying of a deficiency of the wife to win friendship.

Some men sleep with their wife's sister (sister-in-law) thus committing sodomy.

Some men like to put a "leash" on a woman by laying some rules so that she will not have friends, who he is afraid, will open her eyes to the real world lest he loses her.

Some men may be in friendship with a woman or may have a child by a woman, who the woman may be plodding for marriage, but the man keeps giving excuses; such a man is afraid of responsibility or may not be in love enough to keep a marriage. Marriage carries a man or woman to greater responsibility and any man not prepared for this will never be a good husband. If a woman has a child by such a man, she may find herself redundant.

The more a man gets into the limelight, the more women will be attracted to him. Take a look at basketball players and musicians or a celebrity — the world hails them with applause.

Some men like to turn a woman into a doormat where they wipe their feet.

Some men use women to release dynamic tension and once they get the satisfaction they want, they wouldn't see her any more.

Some men marry a woman as a "Ford Pinto", but expect the service of a "Lincoln Continental."

Some men like everything they do very small. At the supermarket they would buy the smaller bottle of jelly. At car dealership they would buy a Ford Pinto instead of a Lincoln Continental because that is too expensive. They are extremely "tight."

A man who is too particular about his money will never find a woman to live with him.

Some men, married or unmarried, feel that a woman belongs to them only at the time of sex. Thereafter, she belongs to someone else.

The taste in sex is so strong and powerful that it can make a man promise a woman Heaven where he himself doesn't know where it is. The best for a man is to be quiet during the performance until the game is over.

Some men build invisible fence around a woman so that she will not see well thus keeping themselves as the only "focus."

For some men, when you are paving their road with bitumen for them to travel on, they are secretly digging pot holes for you to fall into because they are jealous of your good character.

How a man can ward off temptation: Develop a "mental button" that you must always press "Be wise" when confronted with a weakness, say to have an affair with another person's wife or to steal from another:

1. Develop a "nail principle" that one must use when weakness faces him. Turn it into a nail that protrudes wood so that when it is hit on the head, it goes straight into the wood.

There are two kinds of men: First one is completely animal. He does things without conscience or walks over other people without compassion — very wicked; a murderer or a thief — a bad man;

2. Second is completely human. Does things with feelings. Cares about others and is guided by conscience when he does things — a good man.

Some men have more feminine qualities dominant in them than in other men. They are the kind when confronted with some mishap or difficulty cry immediately. They like to dabble in self-pity. They blame someone for their mistakes. A little fight brings them into pieces. They are the cowards and the weak ones.

Some men have more masculine qualities dominant in them than in other men. They are very brave and cut through problems with precision and have no time to tolerate or be patient in situations. They are never afraid to go to great heights.

Weakness of a man: Man becomes easily corrupt in three great weaknesses that are obvious: money, sex, and alcohol. His desire for such tastes must be trained and controlled. A man with strong principles and self-discipline will not submit to such desires. Sex is a "ball" usually thrown to men in high positions. Those who are alert are never caught, but those who are morally weak are the ones who lose their position by it. To be a worthy man, one has to earn money. People who get to top places must watch their pockets so that "cheap" money does not find its way into them. The lure of money or get-rich-quick will always knock on a man's door, but developing principles and discipline help avoid it. Remember! Three things every man must prevent: 1. Wrong money; 2. Wrong sex and 3. Alcohol as a companion.

Some men talk about sex as a prowess to show their manhood and the many women they have gone with or won on their plate and how many miles they can go in energy. Some turn women into a basketball, playing with her as they wish and then tossing her to another man.

Some men combine their sex drive with alcohol. The fall of a man from great height comes as a result of any of these qualities. Knowing how to prevent one from being caught in any of these woes is paramount. Sex is for procreation, and the pleasure derived from it must be contracted; otherwise it is a violation of a woman's right and an insult to God.

Good Qualities for a man to develop:

> *The right thing is the signature of God.*
>
> —*Pius Yao Ashiara*

1. Believe in God and in himself as a great man and nothing else.
2. Everything he will do must have the signature of God. He must always ask himself if what he does has the signature of man and God. When a secretary writes a letter for the boss, she reads it over and over again. Then she edits it making sure the tone is inviting and the choice of words are the right ones, and she questions it, "Will this get my boss's expected approval before signature?" If she is satisfied with it, then she can give it to the boss for his signature. So must he do everything for God's signature as true man.
3. He must not limit himself nor change into any other thing than a man with creative powers and strength to develop as a man.
4. Every man must make an agreement with himself and God that he will not go astray and refuse to be bought by any false influence of society.
5. To be an extraordinary person, a man must believe in himself and believe in hard work, perseverance and persistence and patiently wait on his result for tomorrow.

When a man comes in to a spotlight, he faces the whole world. Through the crowd a man asserts himself, "I will be the president." "I will be a star musician." "I will be a great evangelist." "I will become a star golf player." "I will become a star basketball player." When you come to such a height, all eyes are on you and the Press becomes an eagle that is hungry looking for food. It is interested in what you gained in your applause, and it will be interested to report your failures faster, because that is the most delicious food for the press.

Oftentimes, men fail to watch out when they climb so high in their career or they reach the spotlight. They let little weaknesses like bribery, sex, or drink takes the place of wisdom. Many times women come with lipstick, long nails, the best hairdos, and elegant dressings to attract you or woo you on an expedition. When little things like that take over their careers, they turn to beat on themselves, "It is my fault. I should have known better," but then it is too late.

A man should know that when he becomes President, he is sitting on a chair that belongs to nearly 300 million or more citizens, each wanting to sit on it at the same time with him. The White House is turned into a glass building, and people become watchdogs, viewing you through this transparent glass house to bring out your faults, while the media is waiting with a pen, computer, paper, and, perhaps, the law to chew you up. If your underwear is dirty and they see it, is a good meal for the media, all your activities and your life become a see-through mirror. They expect you and your wife or family to be monks, if not saints. Don't gamble with your name and record. You will need them in the future when you want to marry or hold a public office.

THE POLITICAL CHAIR

How can we get the best person to rule us? Many times a native asks this question. Many countrymen and women ask this question. Citizens, residents, immigrants, visitors – all ask the question. All nations worldwide ask this question. It is the political leadership question. It is only one chair and authority leadership. Divine rules are attached to this chair. And that is why the incumbent must take an oath with a Bible to promise before a whole nation and God before beginning its work. It is not a position to seek wealth. It is a position that leaves a person's name in history. If the incumbent violates its laws, he or she faces humiliation or bad name or ultimately death. If you would rule a nation make sure to have two things in mind: the welfare of its citizens and the progress of the nation at large.

Behold! If you take it and turn it into a dinner plate or a two-sided table, top and bottom, to earn your living, you face danger in the future, and the whole world will disgrace you.

Excuse me! Excuse me! Excuse me!
Country men and women! Citizens! Residents! Immigrants! Visitors!
Let me have your attention! Hear me! Hear my speech! Hear my speech right! Listen to my speech.
Open your ears to hear me!
There is only one Chair.
There is only one President's Chair.
There is only one chair at the top of our Government.
There is only one chair for a Senator.
There is only one chair for a Governor.
There is only chair for a Mayor.
It is only one chair – and that is all we have.
It is a holy chair and cannot be held with "dirty hands."
It is a very hard chair, but it has soft sides to hold.
It is decorated with purity, but it has thorns that hurt.
It is a chair of Responsibility.
It is a chair of Accountability.
It is a chair of Hard-work.
It is a chair of Sweat.
It is a chair of Money.
It is a chair of Trust.
It is a chair of Honesty!
It is a chair of Truthfulness!
It is a chair of Courage!
It is a chair of Pride!
It is a chair of Hope!
It is a chair of tomorrows!
It is a property that belongs to millions upon millions of citizens,
But only one person sits on it for only a short duration of time.

It was acquired with human life!
It was acquired with human blood!
It was acquired through bravery!
It was acquired with perseverance!
It was acquired through unity ⁻ that makes it a Sacred Chair.
It was acquired with human love!
It was acquired with boldness!
It was acquired with human efforts!
It was acquired with unity and with rules attached.
It is a chair to be taken with pay.
It is a chair to be taken voluntarily without pay by choice.
It is an honest chair to be sworn to by the Bible
and to the nation and its citizens.
It is the spirit and soul of the masses.
It is the spirit of America Republic.
Behind our currency we embossed "IN GOD WE TRUST."
We rip our nation apart if we take money or a gift for the work.
It is an invisible chair embedded with divine laws.
It is a chair that does not reward but leaves the incumbent's name
in history after death.
A clean Conscience! Reverence! Honesty! Bravery! Courage!
and a trust in God the qualities that make it a Sacred Chair.
Let the honest person step forward to be elected our political leader.

—*Pius Yao Ashiara*

When you become a star golfer, all hands come with applaud, and the media sings your glory, lifting you high for the world to see.

Conversely, this is a danger zone you are standing on. You must be on the watch with wisdom. Many times, if you are not careful, money and sex will trade places with the golf ball. They raise you so high to forget about golf ball, and the vices become more intense on you.

The pleasure derived from sex usually, for some men or women, lasts only few seconds, but the joy becomes so intense and keeps the participant so much afloat, they forget that other pleasures, like good name, pride, are much more lasting. The media is always looking for a drink to sate its thirst. You get caught when you are not cautious.

What a man leaves behind: Driving through our major streets and our neighborhoods, one finds names on streets, signs, monuments, colleges, universities, corporations, and even amusement parks, all catching our eyes. These were the men whose noble deeds have done something for America or the world. These are the men who have done something in history and left their marks on posterity.

It is said that behind every successful man there is a woman, and here comes woman.

Chapter 2
WOMAN

Woman! Now that the door is opened for you, please enter. Walk through the crowd and you will find empty front seats. Sit on one and rediscover you. "Let's go, woman!"

Woman and Beauty: God has made a woman in such a way that she wouldn't have to do too much for beauty to be accepted by a man. Like flower, she already comes with beauty. She likes to bloom when outdoor and always shooting with fragrance.

Let us check with the hair salons and see how many visits have been made there. At home she must have a dresser and mirrors through which she must be reading and looking at herself. Let us watch the changing style with her dresses. She is afraid to wear the same dress twice lest she becomes the "joke" of the day. Take a look at the TV news women. See if they repeat their dresses twice in the week. Their wardrobe must be seasonal with different colors of dresses.

What about their shoes? They are never satiated with what they have. Like Mrs. Marco they must build it into shoe stores to be satisfied.

Woman is the holiest being on earth. From her the human is formed. She is born a woman and nothing else. Anything otherwise is a mockery to God. Any other way she lives other than a woman blasphemes God. A woman is created differently from a man. She is born with vagina and breast – the source of human birth. Her vagina is a sanctuary and cannot be entered without her permission and respect. If she were a Christian, before approaching the pulpit or an altar she would have to make a token bow in reverence, and so must she preserve her productive instrument.

DIFFERENT KIND OF WOMEN:

Most women prefer a home with a house maid or a nanny.

Some women do not take time to study a man before going to bed with him. And before they know it, they are pregnant. They may also repeat this same mistake in their next encounter with another man and before they know it they are pregnant again by another man.

Some women talk and pride themselves about how successful their men or husbands are. They like to discuss his high-ranking position; he is now the senior vice president with its trimmings. He now has the opportunity to travel with the corporate jet, and so on.

Some women talk in large terms of what kind of properties their boyfriends or husbands own. "We just bought a 600-acre property near the ocean — a beach house — with cash." He last year bought a house for his mother with cash.

When it comes to "table talk" about their husbands and the conversation comes to what kind of education they have acquired, she would say, "he has a High School education and wouldn't want to go any further, and I don't have a college degree either, and we have three children; I don't know what to do. We are in the same spot and never move forward."

Some women are gold- or diamond-diggers. They want the best and biggest and most expensive items in the home without caring about the income of their husbands or partners.

Some women do not respect men. This happens when a woman is more educated or has a better source of income coming into the relationship.

Some women who are very beautiful take advantage of their beauty and like to "walk over" men in making choices. They see one and look him over with eyeglasses and say he is not good; the next one is not good enough, and the third one: "I don't like him. He is not my kind."

Some women like to gossip. In the workplace if they go to the next co-worker for a five-minute question, it becomes an hour conversation leading to the discussion of a hairdo or dress of a fellow employee or male's suit or necktie or workplace affair.

Some women are very fast and "bang" on men here and there without thinking about how much they take from their pockets. Some say, "Let me eat small."

Some women are finger pointers. "I am nobody. Let Mrs. Johnson be the president of the PTA. I don't think I am that good to hold that position. I cannot make a speech like Joann.

Some women I call "I am myself and I do not give myself to any man. I don't need a man to take care of me; that is why I went to college. I don't want any man to come and order me around. My mother always told me to get an education so that I can always support myself without counting on a man" — unfortunately when it comes to sex she cannot do that to herself without a man.

Some women are very gentle and weak and defenseless. If they have children with a man and they are abused, all they say is because of the children they cannot leave the relationship or the marriage. They turn the relationship into a tree under which they only enjoy the shade on a hot summer day.

Some women are extremely slow and take forever to do anything, not worrying about an appointment. They take one dress and change it for another, and the pair of shoes is the same — not sure of what to wear. They find only one pair of the shoe and don't know the place of the other one. They would ask the husband, "Do you remember I wore this shoe last month to John and Anna's anniversary? Where did I put it?"

For some women, money is their catch. Once a man has it, they will be available to him. But if he fails to provide as they need, they leave. For some, it is the look of a man. If he is good looking, they don't care about his worth;

Some women like to take the place of men. They like to assert their courage and boldness to the chagrin of a man. They like to be the "boss." When they go with the man with money, they go with all their "teeth" to chew enough off him.

Some women love material possessions. They will buy and buy until the credit cards are warped and eventually rejected.

Some women have what I call "side dish" men. They use such men for recreation and financial emergencies.

Some women are very neat in appearance but very dirty in character. They will explore every kind of man on this earth, and they are never satisfied with what comes to them. If they are given a finger, they don't want a finger but a whole hand.

Just as some men, some women are liars and can lie upon anything. They would keep a straight face without the slightest compunction and lie about anything and possibly swear upon God to cover any wrongdoing;

Some dress so well with a lipstick that tells every man they are "hot" and ready for a march.

Some are "item losers." They lose their husband's money or an expensive item.

Some women go with a man to find out if he is looking for an "overnight ride" or someone good to marry.

Some women are shoe lovers. They will buy every kind and style on the market. Whether the heel is high or low, they will go for it, even if they will limp in it.

Some are men users. They like to get out of a man 100 miles to a gallon, and they will do anything to get the maximum of what they put into the relationship, or they will take a man for a soccer ball and dribble him into scoring many goals.

Some do not respect men in authority or position and consider them equals or that it is their time to assert their womanhood, to show that they can also be leaders.

Some, when they are in their "period" are turned into a tiger. A little thing upsets or offends them.

Some are everywhere when they have a little authority. These I call "Miss All-over." Authority consumes them in such a way as if they were ready to lift the world on their heads.

Some women's love is beautiful and eternally filled with honey and a clean heart.

Some women who wished they had children but never got the chance can be very obnoxious and severe; a little "dirt" in another's home with children is disturbing to them.

Some know that to reach a man's heart is through the stomach, so they make the best meals to keep attached to the love they wish to have.

When a woman wears a "wild expression," some men fear to marry her; they prefer to have her for rides than marriage – their assumption is that she will not make a good wife. She will be more concerned with her material possessions and beauty than being a good wife.

Some women may have a bed provided for them, but they would prefer a mat. In the home she came from, no one worried about a bed; mat was good enough. Her mother never went to college, but she was a good wife and a mother and never extended herself too much, and that was okay for the father.

The second place given to women has left many behind. Some women are still in a fog until others begin to help them or they remain so. Society has programmed them not to believe in themselves.

Some are good cooks and enjoy cooking for the family and she ensures the family doesn't run out of food.

Some women are heavy drinkers. They can talk about any kind of wine and how much they can drink of it.

Some women are greedy and would want more of anything.

Some women, when they have the support of a man, would never do anything to forward their own affairs. Thus, she remains permanently under a man's influence and guidance of a subordinate role.

Some women who are self-supporting care less about the presence of a man in their lives. Those with one or two children in a previous relationship turn their children into a "spouse" and don't look to a man for companionship.

Some women like to be mothers with many children surrounding them. Some love children and like to have many and to see the children come around dinner time with plates asking for more food while the nose of some is running down with sinus while another wets her diaper with another losing or breaking her dinner plate. "Mommy I want more cheeseburger," they would ask. They are not satiated with children.

Some women like to keep their husbands home by preparing good meals all the time and providing all needs for her husband so that he will not have the chance to slip into another woman's hands.

Some women when hard pressed for money seek out a man for sex as a payoff for any financial help offered by a man — this can come from a single or married woman. A situation she seeks to ease her financial needs.

Just like men, some women, spend now, but pay later.

Some women are a windshield wiper for a man so that they can see ahead.

Some women like to proclaim their marriage problems, aloud, so others know what is going in the relationship.

Some women are extremely jealous and can be very evil or spiteful.

Some women cannot hold on to secret ideas and are often excited when matters reach their eyes and ears.

Some women prefer dating married men as opposed to dating single men. They consider those cleaner.

For some women labor and childbirth is a difficult time. They experience extreme pain during labor and childbirth.

How serene is a woman's face? When she is sleeping, a man must look into her face and see how serene and calm the face is and give her that calmness every moment.

When a woman becomes a mother, she has more self-denial in providing for the family than herself. She will many times run out of food for herself after serving the family.

When a woman becomes a mother and a man is absent, she takes on all responsibilities to do the yeoman's work.

At times a woman becomes childish, when men sweet-talk her into sex without considering her age or standing among women.

When the family decides to invite people over, some women in the home, at times, refuse to do any cooking. Many times she considers it too much work for her thus suggests take-out.

Some parents warn their daughters against marrying a particular man. If they did marry, he will never be a good provider.

Some women are also "authority brokers." They like to order their men around.

Some women turn a relationship into a trailer or a dog so that a man is a follower — especially when she is beautiful.

Some women fail to develop some qualities of man that could aid them later in their personal lives. They are women and must remain women.

Some women put a twisted rope into a relationship so that a man is tied into one spot.

Just like some men, some women are shoplifters. A visit to store or a friend's home finds something.

Some women who are in a "good standing" turn to see a man in her relationship as worthless.

Some women are torchbearers or a guiding light for a man. She is always looking for ways and means for her man to keep growing.

Some women are nagging, morose and shrewish and are careless homemakers.

Some are cowards and like to wear soft shoes around a stern man or husband, so that they will not step on his toes.

Some hold their beauty very high. While she is pursuing beauty, she must develop character that is stronger than beauty so that in a relationship a man cannot leave her after her beauty is gone. With a woman choosing a man for a relationship, she must determine two things about him. "Is he ambitious and conscience and a good thinker with wisdom?" This must be her question.

A woman may have a child or two with a man in their early years of the relationship, where the man failed completely to make the best of himself. But a wise a woman, because of her children, will try to train her man so that he will be there to help raise the children. If a woman focuses on his deficiency rather than training him, she will lose more than the man; besides, her children will grow up without a father, which will not be good for the children's future.

With some women, every time they form a friendship with a man, the next thing they know he fades out of the picture and another chance is gone. With some women, when a man goes with them, he stays for only a short period of time. They take another one, and he disappears. Why such things happen to them may be that something personal about them is repellant. In such a case, a woman must study herself to find what is wrong, it maybe she does not use perfume or a kind of perfume she uses or a body problem. A thorough personal investigation should help end that repellant.

A woman turns to be bitter when some injustice is done to her man or her husband, and she likes to retaliate.

Some women in a relationship with a man turn it into a car and let her mother drives it her way. This is common in marriages.

Most women treasure their children more than their breath. They will go to any length to provide for them, and their good is always at their heart. This is the greatest desire of mothers.

When a woman is in difficulty and she is in a relationship and seeking help from a man, she is more humble and respectful.

Unlike a man, some women can stay away from sex for many years and will not yearn or care for it.

When a woman is angry in a relationship the way she punishes her partner or spouse is to sleep at the edge of the bed with the back turned to her man. If she is touched, she becomes a tiger.

A woman is like a door. If it is not opened, no one can enter. For the wrong or right to take place in sex, it is the willingness of a woman. No man can force it on a woman if she definitely rejects it except in rape.

A woman's looks at times, rather than her character, holds a man in place. And the woman who knows how to use her beauty wins a man.

Some married women may have an outside relationship with another man where she becomes pregnant, then brings the child to her marriage without the husband knowing. This brings child of a different man into a marriage. This is a wrong done by some women in marriage.

Some women have "good teeth" and know how to get more out of a man, turn him into a shish kebab on a pick, and pull the meat off one bite at a time until everything is finished off the pick and before a man knows he is left a pick without meat and it is too late for him to realize it.

Woman and her children: Pain suffered at childbirth and the work involved in raising children make children very dear to a mother.

A mother will do anything for her children to become somebody even if a man is not in the picture. Her pain and suffering make children dear to her.

Women are on the competition platform now. If you watched the Olympic game that recently took place in London, women from all over the world came to compete with each other in a particular sport. Woman has realized that she was told yesterday she will not amount to anything better than a wife or a housekeeper, but she can take a leadership by self-development without reaching to a man for her needs. Now she can also win a gold or bronze medal. The Olympic

Game became a searchlight for mostly a woman to rediscover herself. Gabrielle Douglas did so well at the Olympic Games she was nicknamed the "flying squirrel."

By nature a woman is a jealous person. She becomes more jealous when her contemporaries' or friends' marriages are working and her own has problems. She, at times, aspires her marriage in the same place.

Women are more careful drivers. To turn to the next lane they take extra care and attention before they switch lanes. When turning left or right to the next street they turn to be slower. Many of them find it difficult to make parallel parking. They will look for another space to park instead of spending time to parallel park.

A woman who acts like a man, who shows off she can do it all alone, drives men away from her because men prefer a woman who is feminine and a woman not one that assumes a man's role. Men want a woman that is submissive and not a "boss."

Some women really like sex and desire the strokes that come continually from the penis keeping them afloat with captivating joy and like to go as many times their energy can take them.

Some like expensive clothes and buy several and charge them to a credit. They bring the clothes home and try them on for a few days and return them with the excuse "they didn't fit."

Some use night gown or robe to charm a man to sex. They come dangling in a man's presence to provoke him to an erection. Some keep their pubic hair bushy or overgrown to draw a man's attention to sex.

Some women never learn to stand on their own and when the man they lean on pulls out, they come to grief.

When a woman has a man or is married, but interested in another man, she talks down her existing man or husband to gain the acceptance of her new interest. "Oh, my husband does not give me money anymore or he wouldn't sleep with me anymore — he has lost interest in me," she would say.

Some women mothers are Cover Sheet for their daughters and wouldn't want any man to approach them.

Some women grade the size of a man's penis. They often remark, "He was bragging about that if he ever had me in bed, he would tear me into pieces, but when he came around I thought he was carrying much in his lap, disappointingly, his is a little tiny thing not worth much. I wasn't impressed," they would remark.

Some women are, at times, in two places in a relationship. Deep down in their hearts they know they won't go far with a man, but they make, as a ploy, the top look good.

Some women who have children by a man of whom they did not get much, condemn the man in their children's presence. They would say they don't need a man, but this a mistaken belief. Everyone in this world needs somebody. You need the grocery store owner for your milk. You need an emergency crew to take you to hospital in an emergency. You don't have all the hands of everyone in the world. You have only two hands that are all you can get and live by.

Some women lament when they can't have children and are in pain every time. God gives such women a sick husband to test them if they ever had a child and how they would handle him.

Many women in relationship with a man look only on the icing and do not look to their own future when they go into a relationship and later realize it when it is too late.

Some women sleep with their sister's husbands and in some instances replace themselves in the marriage.

Women in many marriages turn to outlive the marriage. Their husbands may end up dying first.

Some women (mostly wives) have the tendency to discourage or derail their ambitious husbands who want to go into a venture for himself instead of working for some other person. These wives are afraid that their husbands may fail and would rather settle for the status quo. The first question she would ask when the husband brings up the topic of self-business or a venture, "What would happen to the mortgage, the car payment if the business didn't succeed?"

Some women think they put a "leash" on a man when they have kids by him and they continue having many kids until the man disappears to their dismay.

Some women, once they are married and are comfortably provided for they don't worry about growth or their future. They throw themselves into a man's lap and sit there complacently like a baby until something happens to the husband before they would be awake. If a man complains all they would say "I am your wife; you have to care for me."

Some women like to have children by different men. Each of her children must come from a different man.

A woman whose marriage has failed through a divorce, death of a spouse, or through an unexpected break or other can become very bitter and disillusioned with other married partners or with life in general and be turned into a flame snarling viciously at anything that draws near her gets burned.

When a woman's relationship or marriage with a man is not working, she becomes frustrated and bitterly angry thus turned into an empty container on top of a river flown around trying to hit anything.

The greatest salesperson on earth is a woman. She got the title on the day she convinced man to eat the forbidden fruit in the Garden of Eden. Thus any woman born to this earth assumes this curse.

Many a woman does not care whether a man paid her air fare from Brazil to the United States of America or paid all of her father's funeral expenses that will attach her love to him. She does not look back on the good things that happened yesterday. She is interested in what is on the plate right now.

Many a woman, when it comes to a relationship or marriage, look at the opportunities and advantages that will come to her in the relationship before she accepts the union. She is usually imaginarily married to the best in a man before the physical engagement takes place.

Just as some men, many women are like seed in the soil. They receive rain or water, sunlight and air, but they refuse to grow despite the plodding from their partners or husbands. They remain like that until they stagnate.

Some women are "cheats" on men. When things are going well in the home and milk and honey are in enough supply that is when there is smile on the face. "Woe betide" a man difficulties arise! She makes all kinds of remarks. "He wouldn't look for a full time job and he is wasting time trying to invent a 'motor bike,' a thing many attempted and failed that has become his focus and hope. Last month we couldn't send the mortgage payment and last week the Gas Company shut off our gas system; this week we received a warning from the Electric Company if payment is not made within a week they were going to shut off that as well. Now I have to move into my parents' home with our three children and I don't know what to do." Be careful! For many women, if a man's attempt in building a typewriter that never become a computer or boat that never become a ship, a machine that never become an airplane, her man is considered a loser. His home is followed by all kinds of remarks from the wife. "He spends a few hours on his project during the day and sleeps the rest of the hour, but at night, when the family is sleeping that is what he works on at night disturbing everybody.

Some women fail to drive. They believe God never made them to be drivers. Once the first attempt to drive derails them in snow they wouldn't try it again. They are afraid to make any effort further.

Some women who have no children turn material possession into that desire.

A woman may be at the height of fame yet she can be naïve by sleeping with a teenager without thought to self-respect or her marriage — this is a blatant weakness of woman.

Some women can turn a man who is really in love with them around like a pillow not knowing which side to sleep on. In such situations, a man becomes woman's "joke."

Some women when there are financial difficulties in a relationship, they fail to look on the future of the relationship, but seek its immediate solution by sleeping with another man for a relief.

Some women treasure their vigina as money-making apparatus and will use it freely without regard for a loathsome disease or self-respect and that leads them into prostitution.

A woman admires a well-dress man with a neat appearance.

Many woman pay attention to their kitchen and guest dinner plates, forks, spoon, table mats so that when guests visit it provokes envy.

When a woman trains her mind when young a man's penis cannot derail her.

Some women value their vigina as goldmine. If Mr. Fox didn't pay for it, Mr. Right will willingly offer a higher price for it.

In marriage, some women have double-mind: one is for selfish reasons and the other is to "play around."

Many women are like brassiere, all the same, because all brassieres go to hold the breast and only differ in color and sizes.

Some women, if they want to punish or curse or possess a man completely, wash off their "vigina" with water and use the residue water to cook for him. This is a woman's spiritual power of capturing or getting at a man.

The taste in sex is so strong and powerful that it can make a man promise a woman Heaven where he himself doesn't know where it is. The best for a man is to be quiet during the performance until the game is over.

Kill all women and you destroy humanity.

— *Pius Yao Ashiara*

Investment in a Woman: When you invest in a woman you have a future capital at hand. Woman is beauty and her beauty creates the cosmetic industry, the sewing companies, the jewelry companies, the shoe companies and the beauty salons. When she shares her life with a man she produces a product, a man and woman. Her creative talent is unimaginable. Raise a woman well and the world grows.

For a future marriage to work well it is advisable to take a partner from the bottom of life and both build it from scratch. In that way, each invested much into the relationship and may be interested in its security.

A good woman is a great wife and an excellent mother and wonderful grandmother. A great woman learns from other important great women of the world. She learns how they came about their greatness. She would learn from the blind woman Helen Keller, Michelle Obama, Hilary Rodham Clinton, Secretary of State, Former Secretary of State Condolezza Rice, Judge Judy, Gloria Allred, Opera Winfrey and the wives of our presidents and women administrators.

A woman with tenacity: Woman endures pain more than man. She fights through childbirth, and this makes her more resistant to pain. During the winter, the cold weather bites all trees, but the trees accept its presence and obey, but they never move from their way or spot. A tree says, "Here I stand, and I am not moving an inch. Do whatever you want with me, and leave me alone. I have force and power within me you cannot take away. I will prove this to you at springtime. Take all my leaves; I will replace them to your surprise. I am a tree with resistance. I am very firm and bold and hold my ground. This is the kind of strength and courage that a woman has, and she should always maintain it.

A woman who likes variety: There are some women I would call "aunt variety." Like different kinds of dishes one likes to taste, so they look for different kinds of men with different kinds of penis – short and long ones who can anchor them and take charge of the show. Such women like to feel the force and thrusting of penetration under which they scream with all kinds of "come-on; let's go!" for the performer, which some of them call "superman."

Woman and lonely moments: When a woman is in a relationship for 10, 20, 30, or more years, and her partner or spouse comes home and tells her, "Honey, I am sorry I want out of this relationship," or a man in a loving relationship suddenly dies, it puts an arrow into a woman's heart. She turns to seek peace and tranquility that will bring her momentary oblivion. Some turn to hate a man forever. Others hold onto the memory of the love one that died. They find the pain too excruciating when the husband is dead and the children are old and never come to see mamma. Every woman must first understand that there are uncertainties in life and Providence will not give every person one hundred percent joy and happiness and every life will end one way or the other. It is good to prepare for the vicissitude of life.

In your early years of relationship you should seek love, trust, honesty, and reliability. These four qualities are the bond that keeps us attached to each other. If you cannot determine or find these qualities in a partner, there could be some danger to the relationship in future. We all have to study marriage and each other like an equation to make a good meaning out of it.

Chapter 3
MARRIAGE

Questions you ask yourself before marrying!

The marriage vow is a carriage when
broken the pieces are hard to put together.

—*Pius Yao Ashiara*

1. Do you know, in it, there is a place for God?
2. Do you know and understand marriage?
3. Do you know its faults and is a thing of the *heart*?
4. Do you know that it is the greatest institution and corporation on earth?
5. Do you know its disrespects, aggravations, aches, pains and hurts?
6. Do you know is for faithfulness, honesty, trust and loyalty?
7. Do you know what True Love means?
8. Do you know that adultery in it is tantamount to murder and death?
9. Do you know it entails financial difficulties, hardships and sickness that need to be worked out by the two people?
10. Do you know children are the most important beings in marriage?
11. Are you willing to build your LOVE into a bronze statue?
12. Are you willing to hold onto it "for better or for worse until death?"

Before we marry, we must first learn about love. What it means to love. We should not be drawn by the lipstick on a woman's lips or the height of a handsome-looking man alone. We must reach what is called love, which then becomes the path of our journey of marriage. Love is the concrete foundation to good marriage. Be patient! True love does not grow rapidly. It does not burn with flame; it smolders. Love is also a very wild animal with changing moods. True love hesitates. Its hands and feet are slow and do not like to be hurried.

Bring Your Love

Give me a home in your heart with your love,
But not cry at my death.

Bring warmth to my heart with your love,
But not weep at my funeral.

Lay a wreath on my heart with your love,
But not shed tears on my grave.

—*Pius Yao Ashiara*

Congratulations, bride and bridegroom! I salute you, husband and wife. The bell has rung for you both; march on. March on with confidence. March on with enthusiasm. March on with hope. Your life and happiness are before you. Enjoy them!

The important ingredients for a successful marriage are total commitment, good communication, and compromise. Marriage is a unique field, just like a basketball game with opposing players with goals to win. One must be totally committed to score winning goals. When in the field, nothing else is important than winning, and so should be marriage when contracted. It is like an airplane just landed. Some husbands and wives are getting off, but some new mates are not looking at the risk involved and, with promises to each other, are getting on to take the ride to the Land of Happiness and wish to earn the degree of Dr. Happiness. It must be the desire and goal of the two people to build the marriage into a hut or into an Empire State Building. Both must determine that. Beware! A husband and wife are like the human hands — left and right. Each takes care of the other.

Marriage is a goal, and we must set a goal when we go into it. A good marriage is "Take and Train or Educate One Another."

Love in friendship between a man and woman is an objective to work on towards a goal in marriage. True love is a seed that takes time to grow. Love is a seed that needs to be watered with constant attention and care; otherwise it will atrophy. A man must give himself three conditions to meet before thinking of marriage. When we apply for work with a company, many require us to take a blood test or medical examination. Likewise is marriage to make sure we have no health barriers. On another hand, a man must think of what kind of education or training he has that will bring him income, because seventy-five percent of marriage success depends on a man – the foundation of the marriage. He must find out if he is a responsible person who is always reaching higher and willing to keep growing in mind as well as financially. We take marriage like an empty balloon. The first time is empty, but we have to put air into it. The amount of air we put into it will determine how much it will inflate and soar into the air. The more air (efforts) there is, the higher and higher it will go, dancing in the sky with signs of "Happy Wedding"; "Happy Marriage"; "Happy Valentine's Day"; "Happy Mother's Day"; "Happy Father's Day"; "Happy Anniversary," and so on it goes. Before we marry, our first prayer to God should be:

"My God, I am on the way to Marriage Land; please help me make the right choice in marriage."

Marriage is a journey of HOPE.

— *Pius Yao Ashiara*

In the Garden of Eden, marriage was created as a paradise. When we marry, we create a paradise. That is why we add music, dancing, meals, photographs, memorabilia, and so on. When we become a husband we come to the second higher place of manhood. Here our problems for a man will increase, because we are no longer one but two. When we are a man, we are only one person and we owe only ourselves. But when we are a husband, we owe somebody else in addition to ourselves. When we become a father, our problems as a father will increase, because we are no longer a husband but a father with a child or children. When we become a father our status will raise us eventually to grandfather.

It is the love, selflessness and willingness that make extra hands in marriage. When we buy a car, we consider price, the quality, and style. We make sure that we are buying something that will last and something that will give us pleasure and joy. So must be our selection of a partner. Marriage is a car traveling "East" to the Land of Happiness. A husband is the driver and a wife is the co-driver taking the passenger's seat next to the driver. The back seat is for the children – all on their way to the Land of Happiness. Once every year, in our own cubicle, we must have a "husband-and-wife" day to celebrate.

The moment we begin to date a woman, we must see if we can find a wife and a mother's heart in her and in turn to see if we can find a husband and a father's heart in him. These findings will be our guide in our future plans in the relationship. Many people enter this institution but never ask themselves this question before entering it. "What is marriage?" *A marriage is a sanctified contract between two adult persons, a man and a woman, coming together with a vow to be one forever in the presence of family, friends, and God.*

It is a sacred institution to be worshipped, respected, and revered. It is paradise on earth the moment it is entered to live and enjoy with songs, music, dance, and praise to God. It is a garden created in black and white colors, the significance of its seriousness and purity. The rules for these colors are strict and cannot be stained. Nothing comes between them nor mixes them with any other color. It cannot be taken without a promise to the world and God! We take it with a ring to our fingers, and that puts us into a ring that is bonded. What happens in the ring cannot be taken outside of it. Conversely, anything wrong outside cannot be brought into it.

The success and failure of every marriage affects society: whether it is consummated in private, in a nook, in a village, in a city, or in a grand ballroom. If it is successful, it promotes happiness, joy among family and the world. If it fails, it creates bitterness and gossip among the two people and perhaps family members and may become an enterprise for lawyers and, of course, the court to feed on.

Marriage equation: $1 + 1 = 2^0 = 1$

It is only in marriage, one plus one is equal to two raised to the power of zero to be one. This is a very difficult math assignment, but real equation to understand and solve by the two friends before consummation. It has to be raised from the bottom through effort and work to bring it to the highest standard to be one.

Figure 1: Marriage is mixing orange juice with apple juice.

Marriage is mixing orange juice with apple juice: Here we go!

We need a stirring stick (which is the years it will take to blend into growth).

Marriage is the greatest investment and a corporation to be undertaken on earth — no other investment equals it. The Chief Executive Officer is the husband and Vice President the wife. Here its products are *human beings* where quality control is very important. If we produce mediocre products, we produce a mediocre society. You hold the hand today we hold it forever. It is a challenge for those who have taken it while the world is watching closely to see what the two have made of it. It is a promise to hold and keep and cannot be broken. Once taken, it is taken forever with joy until the end of both lives.

Many wish if there were a school to study, they would take classes before entering into marriage. It is like wishing to be a swimmer. One consults with an experienced swimmer to understand the intricacies of the river or the ocean.

In marriage, we cannot depend on any outside forces to make it work. A car must run on its engine to travel. The power that is built into it is the only power that will make it work. It is therefore necessary that the two people must understand each other. To be married is to be "involved" from head to toe. Put all the breath inside you into it. Marriage is like a mountain for some. They find the early steps (years) easy, but as they climb further, they can't go any more. Unless life is put back into it, fresh and strong as the wedding day, it will atrophy.

You must take it at the beginning with a book in hand, with everyone writing in a column his or her likes and dislikes. We must turn into book writing and continue editing, adding, putting a comma here, putting a semicolon here, a colon there, a period there and a question mark here, parenthesis around some sentences, and reading and rereading over and over again — asking ourselves, what do we add and what do we take out? How can we make it better? How can we make it into a permanent happiness and joy and remain the same as at our wedding, where our invitees complimented us with kind words, "You look gorgeous," "I like your wedding dress. Who made that for you?" "Look at your husband; he looks so handsome." Turn it into a mirror and keep looking at each other while correcting each other's mistakes and faults with respect. You must become both a teacher and a student while swapping positions. This is the way it must go until death.

At times we take it with a doubt and uncertainty, afraid and not sure if it will work. We vacillate; we wander, and we twirl. We move to left and move to right in our decision, not sure what to do at times.

A man faces a bigger challenge when he holds a woman, a daughter of another man and woman with a lifetime promise. With this promise he invites God as a witness, and he cannot negate its duties.

To be serious in it, we take the vow with a black tuxedo and a white wedding gown with a vow never to stain it in any way. *The vow is the voice of God in marriage. It is the communication and promise link between us and our maker.* We invite hundreds of family members and friends to witness our event. But how many marriages never disappoint such people?

If marriage were a car to test drive, many people wouldn't buy it. If it were a dress or a shirt, we would try it on before buying it. If it were a shoe, we would try it on in all sizes before we picked one. No, No! No! You cannot try on marriage. It will never fit you exactly the way you may want it. That is the way one is to take it and put work and love and happiness into it.

It is not a game to win scores over another person, but a dedicated task with a strong will to succeed with it.

Please take a look at the one hundred dollar bill in the hands. He raised the money high before your eyes. We have faith in money and trust that it will do something for us. It will talk for us and translate our desire into practical purpose. So will marriage. Let anyone walk to him and ask to be given this money if he will be willing to release it. Or give him a waste paper basket or garbage can to throw the amount into it. I can say for sure he wouldn't do that, because he earned it. In his hands it is paper, but the faith he has in it that it will do something good for him is why he holds onto it with tenacity.

This behavior is synonymous with marriage. When we take it with clean clothes with seriousness and holding it high with faith, trust, and belief that we will derive joy and happiness from it, it works.

There is no difference in the purchasing power of money and the retention power of marriage – they all work the same.

A man and a woman getting ready to marry: Marriage is the pillar that makes a man or a woman a solid human being.

Figure 2: "In God We Trust."

Marriage as a foundation to a solid Life

The Law of Marriage stipulates: "Take it, but you can't get out of it."
When contracted, it is contracted forever.
Several lovers don't understand what it means to be married.
Many lovers only take it to be admired as couples; but this is a mistaken desire.
Marriage is a Crown! Reverence and worship adores it.
Marriage makes a person solid.
Human beings are like a tree: That is why they must have roots.
Human beings are like a building: That is why they must have a foundation.
Human beings are only half a person,
But marriage makes them a complete whole.
A husband and wife are a foundation and prop to each other.
With a husband, a wife is his foundation and prop.
With a wife, a husband is her foundation and prop.
Of marriage, there is someone to share your joy and happiness.
Of marriage, there is someone to lean on in time of sorrow.
Take marriage as a white wedding gown with dignity.
Take marriage as a Black Tuxedo with decency.
When they are stained, onlookers want to know why.
Oh, my friends why did it come out this way? This question people ask!
Oh, my brother and sister, marriage is a Sacred Union.

Oh, my brother and sister, marriage is all laughter and joy.
Do not let "dirt" touch it!
Do not let "bitterness" taste it!
Do not take it with regret!
Do not take it by crying in it!
Do not let your mother share its problems.
Do not let your father share its problems.
Do not let your aunt share its problems.
Do not let your uncle share its problems.
Do not let your relatives share its problems.
Do not let your friends share its problems.
Do not let a pastor or a priest share its problems.
Do not let an attorney solve its problems.
Do not let the judge solve its problems.
Do not let the court solve its problems.
Do not let any person share its problems.
This is the right way to keep it serene and peaceful.
Hold it with faith in God.
Hold it with hope in God.
Hold is with belief in God.
Hold it with your two hands.
Hold it by standing on your two feet.
Hold it with courage.
Hold it by telling the Truth.
With reverence hold it carefully as a Crown.
Take it with LOVE which is deeper than the ocean.
Take it by constantly decorating and polishing it.
Take it with joy and happiness.
Take it with pride.
Take it by correcting each other.
Take it with good wishes for each other.
Take it by guiding each other.
Take it with strength!
Take it with tenacity!
Take it by dancing in it.
Worship it!
Stand by it!
Stay in it!
Be on guard by it!
Work on it!
Put "fire" under it!
Do your best with it.
Handle it well to become a lesson and envy for married couples.

—*Pius Yao Ashiara*

Marriage prevents a man or woman from letting the wind carry him all around the world. Without it, a young man or woman is only a hunter, roaming every kind of forest to hunt. Without it a man or woman is only wall and no foundation.

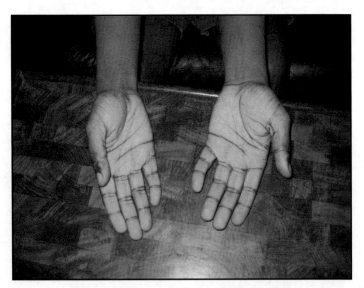

Figure 3: The two palms must be carrying
some form of work before marriage.

Before we marry, we must sit by a table with two chairs: One chair as candidate for marriage and another chair as an interviewer. We must answer all questions we expect the interviewer will ask us, because many people see marriage as a problem rather than a paradise of Eden to plant flowers to turn well and kept. He must give himself a lesson. First is to study human nature, then study woman and her qualities and what makes her happy – this may vary nonetheless. He must stretch his two arms in front of him and look into his palms to ask the question, "What do I have in my two hands to carry me into a marriage?"

If he cannot answer this question, perhaps it is best to suspend his desire until he finds an answer.

Know the kind of man you are and make sure you are right before taking a woman. Decide what lane you want to take. Will it be a fast lane, a middle lane, or a slow lane? The strength you will build into yourself will determine if you are a little fellow or a giant fellow. Unless you turn yourself into a "knock on wood," you will not go far in marriage. A man must be all there to succeed in marriage. It requires the spirit and energy of a good man, a great husband, and a wonderful father and an amazing grandfather. On becoming a good man, one must come from the group of good men. And on becoming a good husband, one must come from the group of good husbands. And on becoming a great father, one must come from the group of great fathers. Remember! Marriage is not an already made shirt or dress you go into a store and try on before buying – it requires selection, studies, work, and love, and many years of patience and tolerance. Marriage has two sides, like a book with a front and back.

The front only shows or sells its goodness; the back side hides its faults. When it is well treated or well built, it brings joy; when it is left to break, it brings hatred and bitter animosity, and its pieces will hurt you. Conversely, marriage is like an ice cream. It has sweetness, and as we enjoy its sweetness, its accumulated years decrease as we move on.

If we will call on all animals and trees or all living things that have life to come forward and ask them by what means they grew, we will hear astonishing stories of varying degrees from each of them.

Men and women think they are the only things on earth with problems. No! Everything that must grow will have some problem to fight. Any move you make to bring a change into your life is a challenge and possibly a change.

When you enter college, the first day of class seems very easy, but as the days and years go by and you begin to climb uphill and more work is required, you begin to feel the pinch. Marriage is the same. The first day is full of joy, laughter, smiles, and happiness. But as the days go by and we begin to discover weaknesses in our mates, we begin to sigh. "Had I known?" We look at yesterday when we made our choices and promises and we begin to wonder why this decision. *Marriage is a journey that looks forward and not backward.* You can look into its rearview mirror for quick reference to build yours, but that should not be your Google, GPS or MapQuest. Every marriage is its own make and style.

Remember! There are three things every tongue likes to speak, every eye likes to see, and every ear likes to hear: "good thing." This should be on your mind during this journey.

When you marry, the staircase of marriage is going to promote you to the next level: a husband. Here your responsibilities will, no doubt, increase and your care and concern will be demanding and stronger. A man must know what a woman expects from him in marriage. A woman, by nature, expects a man to take the front lead. He must be the bulldozer to move the earth. He must keep moving like a river – always on the go. She wants him to be the commander of the "home army." Everyone nearly first learns from his parents. We were born out of a relationship – married or unmarried. We saw treatment of a mother and the treatment of a father. All these lessons or classes were before our eyes, and we know what is good and what is bad when they raised us together.

When he becomes a husband, he may be promoted to a father. Here the responsibilities will triple and more energy will be required.

The dream doesn't end there. Here he will be led to the level of a grandfather who becomes a visiting lecturer or instructor to the next generation of family members. Be a man in marriage with a pride.

He must be aware of the two wildest animals in marriage that may build or destroy a marriage: *love and money*. Given out here in the alphabets, they live next to one another: A B C D E F G H I J K L M N O P Q R S T U V W X Y Z (Love and Money live next to each other and are companions, as well as Love and Marriage go together).

In marriage, train your spouse to train you. When you invest in your spouse, you build a future bank and there is profit to be gained. When he becomes a father, he must develop a "mother's imaginary seat" in his mind and visit from time to time, so that he doesn't become comfortable in a father's seat. Consequently, a wife must develop a "father's imaginary seat" and visit from time to time so that she doesn't become comfortable in a mother's seat. Marriage is shoe swapping between the husband and wife so that everyone feels the pinch somewhere in the marriage.

A man, especially, should be aware of illegal aliens for marriages that "stand tall" and are always trying to enter its territory, e.g., politicians, sport athletes, celebrities, singers, musicians, etc. If a man belongs or fills any of these positions, he must be careful because spectators, cameras, and TV will be waiting on him to make a movie.

A man must be aware that marriage is a balanced scale. If he does not want his wife to grow with him in the marriage, then he should not marry. He must grow by himself to see how far he will get. He will grow as a fruit tree, but he will not bear fruits. He must also be aware that it is human nature not to suffer. Nonetheless, it is a woman's nature not to suffer and a husband must make an allowance for it.

People spend several years going to school. When they graduate, they take another time looking for work. When they find work and they are asked to stay a little late at work, they complain. So is marriage. When we spend time and money looking for a partner and the going gets hard, we do not take time to patiently see to the solution except to look at the Court, which we think will be the best solution. Some partners in marriage instead of holding the marriage with two hands to work best kick it to the ground with two feet. At a certain time, one partner may turn the marriage into a tree just for shade and not love in the marriage but for others to perceive it as a "good marriage."

As a woman, make sure you have a future with a man before deciding on having children out of the marriage or inside the marriage. Remember! Technically speaking, a man does not push a stroller. It is often the woman. A man walks away from a child or children, but mostly women stay with the child or children. A decision is necessary to prevent your child or children from being orphans. *It is too hard for a mother to raise children without a father.*

We must remember! God gives us the days of our lives a second-at-a-time and one-day-at-a-time just like a father will give the daughter one dollar a day for school so that she will not waste them and turn them into a fortune. So our married days must be spent wisely without unhappiness and waste.

A husband must encourage the wife to have some form of education or training. This helps a wife soar higher. Look into the lives of the late Dr. Norman Vincent Peale and Mr. Dale Carnegie. Their wives joined them in their pursuits. When they died they took over their work. A husband should not be afraid in marriage, assuming if things don't turn out right, he would lose. A husband must turn the marriage into a flame and see to it that he is putting in firewood constantly to keep the fire perpetually burning – he cannot be lazy in the marriage. In some cases he may have to go through fire to get water for the family.

In some marriages, it impossible for the woman to have children, and she will be hurting every now and then, especially when she goes into a gathering where there are children or sees a mother crossing the street with her children. He must note that such a wife can be very particular about things. She can be particular or critical about a little mess found in another person's home, because she has never had the chance to be a mother. *A mother's home is dirt and cleaning and washing and cooking.* In marriage there is nothing interesting like having your children around you and each throwing playful punches at you in joy screaming, "Daddy, we are sinking. What are you doing about it? Get the rent in before we are thrown out… before I drop out of school … before we run out of food … it is snowing and we are cold. We need heat."

A husband must understand that it takes some wives to be strong; in such a case, a husband should try to "weight lift" his spouse. She may say, "I am good enough for myself. I don't want to go that far." It is a husband's duty to encourage her to grow. He must be in place for her.

Living is in breaths, and every breath should be a joy and happiness; thus you don't short-change yourself or your spouse when death occurs. A father's bed is not made comfortable. At times he must be in both places: father and mother, and so a mother must be in both places: mother and father. Marriage is changing hands. When we marry, we must begin, immediately, to train ourselves in the double role. Sometimes life's problems or death can combine responsibilities of the two into one.

It is wrong for a father to measure a home life of another mother or couple into his own marriage. It is advisable to tailor your marriage to your own lifestyle and not compare it to another. At times the marriage becomes a trip. One wants to go north, but the other wants to go south. It is always good to sit and discuss things amicably, and as a father, nothing should occupy him more than the marriage.

If you are a father and you ignore your child or children today, you ignore your future and old age. Cane, walker, wheelchair cannot go to the basement to do laundry for you; they cannot go to the grocery store. They cannot drive you around places and to the doctor. It is advisable to put in them all your time and energy while they are young; thus they will become part of you. If you do not make children part of you, they do not know you.

It is good if parents are aware that the time they are raising their children is when they belong to them. After their education or training and they become older and independent, they go to another man or woman, and society also stands at guard taking their time as well. The only time parents enjoy their children is when they are raising them, and that is when their cries, laughter, noise, songs, and music are part of them, which will become their memoir in old age. Children are: "You do for them when young and they do for you when old." Raise them well while young; when they grow up and you become ill or sick and old, then they raise you up. But do not turn them into a pillow to rest your head on, to turn around as you wish.

Some fathers turn to be afraid of their wives when they are too educated or smart or matured. They see her as a gun or any other weapon to wage war when things go wrong. If a man is wealthy, he is afraid she will wipe him out financially if things go wrong.

In marriage, both partners must determine that the marriage takes front page news. If it is a good marriage, society will applaud it, but if it is a wrong one, let society learn a good lesson from it and get a good laugh out of it. Conversely, you can stay in a marriage that has deficiencies and turn it into a school where you can teach each other patiently and slowly to work.

A good marriage is guidance, correcting, tolerance, patience and improvement on yesterday's life of the relationship. In marriage, a good thing to do in correcting a spouse is to correct by showing a polite action, but not correcting the spouse by verbally insulting or beating. Here is a scenario: "A man wore dirty jeans to go out with a friend who called on him in an emergency. The wife didn't like the husband's appearance. She then asked the friend to wait on her husband for a few minutes while she went straight upstairs and took a clean pair of pants and ironed it. She then invited the husband upstairs and politely asked him to change into the ironed pants."

In marriage, everyone is a child, because we have so much to learn, and everyone is a mother and everyone is a father — this approach builds a stronger bond in the marriage.

How the relationship between a husband and wife can turn into different kinds of marriages:

Marriage in Eden: This is the kind of marriage that is properly planned with a goal to reach. A point marked in the marriage to reach. They hold onto the "vow" as promised to each other and seek nothing but its success and happiness. It is an organized marriage that will sparkle like a star in the sky;

Marriage in Hell: This is the kind of marriage that has no direction or plan. The partners went into it just by the name "marriage." It is like trying to affix wood to metal, and there is no happiness but pain, suffering, regrets, and cursing;

Marriage in Pain: This is a relationship left to a mother or father alone. A husband or wife is in it, but just in name. What the French called "marriage de raison" or marriage of convenience;

Marriage in Prison: This is where fear is built into the marriage for selfish and personal reasons for a husband to maintain power and authority in the marriage. It is a situation where a man becomes a Hitler or a tyrant in the marriage, when the wife is cowered into a servant and subordinate rather than a partner or a wife;

Marriage in Sorrow: Where one spouse dies and the living spouse holds onto the ring and their yesterday life together and fails to move forward to a new life. A man, woman, or love no longer means anything to him or her. It is a situation where the heart inside has been totally torn into pieces, and life becomes meaningless.

There are enemies and forces that destroy marriage and some of them are infidelity, adultery, dishonesty, cheating, disloyalty, relatives, friends, and gossips:

Infidelity: Where a husband or wife refuses to call the marriage his or her own with respect to the vow taken to be true and pure and shares it with other outsiders;

Adultery: Where another man or woman is allowed to intrude on the marriage. Or where a husband or wife sleeps with another person outside the marriage for selfish reasons;

Dishonesty: Where one person has not been truthful and the marriage is filled with fibs and falsehood and feeds it only with lies and wrongdoings;

Cheating: Where the marriage has been turned into a discotheque for enjoyment with flirting here and there with different kind of partners;

Disloyalty: Where one or both spouses do not hold onto the marriage strongly with two hands and fail to keep to the promise to each and be faithful in the marriage.

Relatives: Where grandmother, grandfather, mother, father, sisters, brothers, friends, and gossip are part of the marriage.

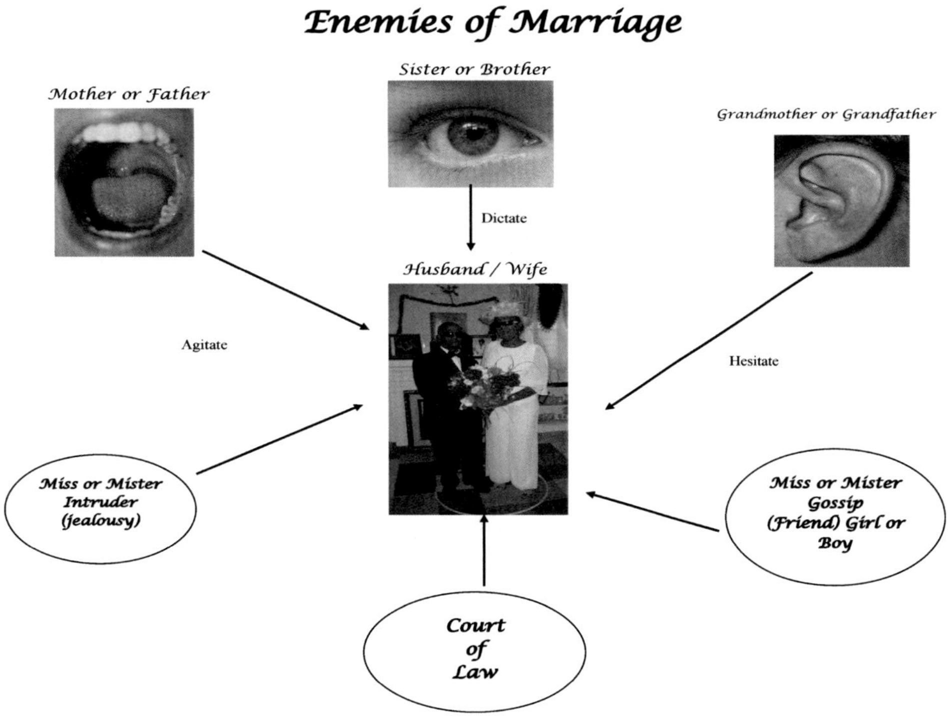

Enemies of Marriage

Figure 4: The Enemies of Marriage.

[Grandfather, grandmother, mother, father, brother, sister, friends, Miss Gossip]

This is what I call: Mother or Father Mouth; Sister or Brother Eye; Grandfather or grandmother Ear; Friends; Miss or Mister Gossip; Mister or Miss Philanderer.

The greatest and bitterest things to avoid in marriage: Adultery and infidelity.

> *Selfishness is a seed that is kept to oneself that never grows.*
>
> —*Pius Yao Ashiara*

Love has beauty as a flower, but it has thorns as well. If you hold it the wrong way, it will hurt you. You cannot share a "married love." Someone said, "Marriage given to me again, I will not take it." [This is a failed marriage where a partner has been severely hurt.] Once you are married, your sex organ becomes a sanctuary. Your vagina becomes a door, and no other person enters it unless your partner; your penis becomes a key and cannot enter any other door than your partner's room (vagina). There is no difference between the person who violates this trust than is he or she a thief, a robber, or a murderer. Adultery is a gun or weapon of any kind put in your spouse's hand to kill, because this is what normally follows this behavior.

Any wrong act that will depreciate the marriage can no longer be called marriage, but called carriage, carrying only two people, but not husband and wife. A true marriage is a mixing bowl, and nothing should be hidden from it. To those who commit adultery in it, married men and women must heed this warning: "Marriage is a seat. You can't knock someone else down and expect yours to stay strong and firm. Don't take the wheel off someone's car and expect yours to run on four wheels. There is no corner to hide from wrongdoing. Your wrongdoing has a kickback, though not immediately rewarded. Everyone's husband or wife is an asset to a marriage. In marriage, always point the accusative finger to yourself when something goes wrong and you will be a good spouse. Marriage is a sanctuary, and no boisterous game can be played on its floor. It has to be kept clean all the time. Why do our parents give us special names? Mary? Christine? John? Peter? James? Michael? And so on? It is because they were people who have done great things and led honest lives. I have never heard anyone called Satan, Devil, but I have heard a person called an angel. So must be marriages kept neat.

When our body is injured and it bleeds and the wound is treated, it heals, but it leaves a scar on the body. But the wound on the heart does not heal easily nor is it forgotten. It is good to avoid one in marriage; the apology, the excuse, "I am sorry"; "It is my fault"; "I apologize" can be said but some traces of hurt remain and can resurface when other painful things happen again in the marriage.

To sleep with someone's husband or wife means you didn't care about your life and you are taking the greatest risk in life. Adultery is animalistic, stealing, murder, and a cardinal sin, and it may bring a weapon to end a life. Marriage is the greatest contract between two people – husband and wife – and the seal that is placed on it is the human heart. At times when an affair is discovered, a spouse may try to mix the affair to conceal and confuse a partner in the wrongdoing, thinking there would be no discovery. The wrong comes out later, because the wrong is never hidden. Here is a scenario: "A young couple has five children: six, five, four, three, and a two-year-old. They had a home, but the woman was a stay-at-home-mom. In order for the man to meet the mortgage and other expenses, he left home early mornings but came back late at night exhausted. Their neighbor, another married young man with children, took advantage of the man's late schedule by sleeping with the wife after he has gone to work. One day, the husband forgot an important document and rushed home to get it. On entering his home, he found his neighbor having an affair with the wife – this had been a long thing going on that the husband didn't know of. The husband had no choice but to ask for a divorce. Here a philanderer has destroyed a marriage of more than six years (many times it happens to 10, 20, 30, 40 years of marriage) with people in the marriage. Now the children are turned into orphans. Where will their mother go from there with five children? What kind of man will want her with someone else's children? If any man would want her, it will only be for sex, where she is good at. Now the husband is faced with two home responsibilities if he decides to marry again. What would have happened in the marriage if the husband did not discover the affair? A child would have been born into the marriage that would not be his, because of his wife's adultery. It could have brought rage to the husband to kill the philanderer, wife, the children, or himself — which could have become a movie for the living. What would happen to the philanderer's wife and family? A broken family as well?

Happiness is right in front of you, but you have to build a foundation for it to enjoy it. To do this, you must develop marriage mirrors to make it stronger:

1. *Windshield Mirror Marriage*: Learn from marriages that are in front of you as your marriage grows;
2. *Side Mirror Marriage*: Learn from marriages that are beside you;
3. *Rearview Mirror Marriage*: Learn from marriages that were behind you before your own marriage;
4. *Back Window Mirror Marriage:* Learn from centuries old marriages.

The beautiful side of marriage comes with beauty, kindness, money, laughter, and smiles, promise-keeping, joy, and happiness, and its love asks for newness all the time — it asks for youth, but at times one has to spoon feed or babysit a spouse in certain things.

At the point of start, a man and woman who decide to marry must turn themselves into a home construction company. They must decide on the kinds of materials they want to start the building. They must build the foundation on

God; the walls must become the husband and wife, and the children become the roof. Children will be the roof anyone far away can see in the future.

Another point they must note is that true happiness in marriage comes in old age of the couple. This is the time marriages belong in the Who's Who Book of Marriage. They must promise each other in the marriage in everything and anything they do must give them only cover pages.

Your marriage should be put on a marriage banner, always to showcase and proclaim the goodness of marriage. Under Marriage Certificate, there is a bigger invisible signature and that is God's signature, which is a debt owed to God. Marriage is a thing in the open and cannot be hidden from the public eye. Your promise and love will, in your eyes, keep your wife or husband looking beautiful every time, because it was not contracted on beauty. It was contracted on your mind and heart. Always find the way to make your spouse happy. *When problems come, solve them among the two of you, and never take your marriage problems to another person to solve. Taking it to another person is like selling your private life — that could be a good laugh for another, though he or she has worst.* In marriage a husband is a barber and a wife is a beautician.

Learn to control your anger in marriage. Any time your spouse angers you, put your ring finger forward and look at it and recite your vow momentarily and say, "For-better-or-for-worst; may peace reign."

The marriage ring is surrounded by pain, selfishness, sorrow, sadness, joy, happiness, infidelity, adultery, jealousy, love, tragedies, disappointments, heartache, headache, and many more, and it is very hard to live in it without meeting any of these problems. Meet them with adaptation. Be a whole person in the marriage with a square around you. When measured, you must fit exactly into the four sides.

You cannot starve your marriage. It must be given food, water, sunlight, air, etc. It must keep growing like the red rose with beauty.

Every father must know that when he is raising children, he is raising husbands and wives, so good work is required of him.

Integrating motherhood: A woman is a salesperson selling her beauty every time. In the marriage, every partner must make him- or herself indispensable. Some mothers are a sharp knife in marriage. If you do not handle them well, and they cut you, it cuts through the Marriage Certificate to bleed. As mothers, we must teach our children to respect and be humble. If you train them well, you highlight them in any group they go into. Make a song for your love and married life that you should both sing every day.

An important thing we must note as mothers is that no matter how high and far we go, in standard we are still women, wives, or mothers and nothing can change that, and the role we play in any of these areas is more important than the standards we want to maintain. We must also note that there is a difference between a wife and a boss – a wife is in the home, a boss is in the office or workplace. In mind, a spouse can drive another out of the home by complaints and nagging. Some partners turn the home into a market with frequent altercations.

You cannot be married and keep holding your parent's wings and flying with them and frequently consulting them for questions and answers to your marriage. This will not make your marriage grow, and it will always be in kindergarten. The moment someone else has to solve your marriage problems, you no longer respect the marriage.

The greatest gift the couple can give each other is "Peace of Mind," especially when a partner is in intellectual pursuits. And the three things that hold the marriage together are:

1. The vow: "For-better-or-for-worst";
2. Love: When they love one another indeed;
3. Children: Children are the heart of every marriage and their presence cannot be ignored when making important decisions that will affect the married life.
   a. If you will leave your marriage, you will look upon your ring and repeat your vow once more;
   b. Your promise to love: You will see how much time, money, efforts, pain, and suffering you put into the relationship;
   c. Where do your children go without a mother or a father? Who else can do a better job raising them than you? You destroy the future and happiness of your children and perhaps make them orphans.

Happiness in marriage is in the future. You cannot find it at the early years of its struggle and growth. You have to work in it to reach it at the summit with many years of work and sacrifices. It takes true living together, doing things together and the hand to hand is necessary for the life of the marriage. It is good when we place a mark on it: "No other marriage shall equal ours." Find something nice to describe your spouse with. Mrs. Thomas Edison described her husband as Nature's Man, but what have you for yours? A husband and wife's bed must be comfortable and decorated. It should be the greatest beauty and comfort in the home. It should be the costliest and greatest investment in the home. This is where their life's comfort should be. After a tired day's work, this is where they must lay their burden. It is a permanent resting place and should be sacredly preserved and be the most comfortable place next to casket and grave.

The ring on the finger is the prize to win in it. Love in marriage takes time and patience to discover a true love.

Marriage "hold-over": There is nothing a man and woman hates more than taking on a problem or work that was not properly done by another person. So are children from another relationship. There are always doubts and uncertainty from both sides of previous wives and husbands. The children may disrespect their stepfather, thinking they will not be treated well with kindness. Their stepfather, on the other hand, may think they are not his children, so he may not get their support and respect he should get, and when they grow up, they will rather turn to their father or mother.

Marriage withers like a flower: On the wedding day we bring flowers to celebrate. But as the days go along, one partner begins pulling out the flowers into an anger basket, thus withering the love that was planted as a seed and eventually atrophies. Trees are a classroom. They live in groups and in a community of a forest. Each lives on its own but takes food from the same soil they all share. It struck its roots deep down and keeps firm. They never borrow nor seek help from one another, and always on their own. But in community they make the forest. Many grow from the stem with two branches, like married couples of a husband and a wife. We should learn from the life of our married lives. A husband and a wife are the beginning of a life, so the foundation they will lay should be strong. It can be turned into rope pulling. It is better to let the one who is pulling be in charge, until fed up, then the next one takes over.

A good wife will be a shock absorber for a husband who is fragile before some specific problems. Conversely, a good husband will be a shock absorber for a wife who is fragile before some specific problems. No marriage is already made. You have to build it from scratch into a car for it to run efficiently. In marriage you let people see only the outside of its beauty. The inside of some of them are too ugly to see and will not encourage others to go in. It is good you don't turn your marriage into an evening story-telling. You belittle the marriage when you do.

What the senses like to do in marriage of others: The eye watches it; the ear listens to its stories; the mouth speaks and tastes it; and people gossip about it. Similarly, you do twelve good things in your marriage, but if you do one thing that violates the Ten Commandments or a wrong is done, it wipes off all the good you have done. Its dress cannot be stained.

The two ways of solving marriage problem:

1. The first approach takes a knife and cuts through it. (Many times the first approach is used by the Court. They try to cut it at the joints, and they cut as they see fit to save time, but this usually results in dissatisfaction of the spouses.)
2. The second approach is turned it into tied rope, which is then patiently untied. (This approach is mediation, where understanding is brought between the two people to solve the problem).

Intrusions: Other women and men study the strength of your relationship with your husband or wife. If it is not strong, they invade it. Outside sex can change the whole course of the marriage. Do not let another man or woman turn your 25, 30, 40 years of love, work, and sacrifices in your marriage into a 15-minute pleasure. Some husbands or wives live in two places in the marriage. The left hand is being dragged by a partner, while the right hand is being dragged by a family member. Human beings are curious, and they may always try to look into your marriage.

There are two types of husbands and wives:

1. One looks in front of him or her to reach his or her marriage goal and happiness;

2. Others look into other spouses' marriage to see the good or bad that is going and keeps talking about it as other than his or her own.

There is no way a man or a woman will do anything and succeed at it without holding it with two hands. God gave us two hands to hold whatever we are doing to succeed at it. But some go into marriage with only one hand and with a half-filled cup and expect to succeed at it. Like a car, hold it with two hands and throw all your energy and attention into it with concentration and drive it forward.

Keeping the Home a Paradise: The two places that human beings live in but spend most time in are the home and workplace. Both ought to be peaceful environments to live, but you may never get it in the workplace as you wish, so home is where *heaven* must be created. Songs, hymns, music equipment must be available for everyday enjoyment, and the home must have a musical theatre, must have a classroom, a growing library with the children introduced to the love of books and reading as obtained in these poems:

> *Lay me to Rest.*
>
> *Lay me to Rest!*
> *Not in the grave,*
> *But amidst books*
> *And I will find my way to God!*
>
> *Leave me alone!*
> *Not with grief and weeping,*
> *But with bookshelves and books,*
> *And I will look for my Destination!*
>
> *Let me leave you!*
> *Not in sorrow and pain,*
> *But build my steps with books,*
> *And that will lead me to Heaven!*
>
> —*P. Ashiara*

Also create an isolated place for everyday worship to God. There the children must be gathered for prayers every day. The home should be a Marriott Hotel and its restaurant. It must be a Holiday Inn. It must be a place of respect and courtesy where children are taught before they go out into the street. The home must be a Heaven. No friction, altercations, quarrels, arguments should be entertained. It must be as peaceful as the cemetery.

We should work hard on our internal qualities to break their habits. External qualities can mostly be corrected after a visit to Nordstrom, Macy's, JC Penney or other stores where their needs can be met.

Marriage is a hard road to travel. Taken with the right attitude, your journey will be a pleasant one. Let your marriage success be the food you eat. The bed you sleep on. The clothes you wear. The shoes you wear. Be the car you drive and the altar where you pray. Let it be the kitchen where you cook. Let it be your mother. Let it be your father. Let it be your sister. Let it be your brother and let it be your friend and let it be your *god.*

Relatives and Marriage: Relatives should be supporters of the married family, but should not be allowed to own it. They should be kind, caring, concerned and share its joys and sorrows but not be allowed to intrude on it.

A failed marriage doesn't mean a failed life. Many times partners do not study each other before going into marriage and later regret that they have made wrong choices. It is good if partners can study each other very well before investing in the relationship. A failed marriage is a drawback for many people, and a lot is lost, just like a bankrupt corporation. They have nothing to show for the relationship except bitterness and hatred.

A woman is never beautiful until she wears a bridal gown; a man is never handsome until he wears a tuxedo. A man and woman are never a couple until the Bible say so!

In conclusion, take your marriage and build it into a pyramid and with God and a victorious attitude and amusement, you will reach Mountain Marriage. Here comes your Marriage Pyramid.

The Pyramid of Marriage
Build it on GOD.
Build it on TRUST.
Be Optimistic.
Always eat at HOME.
Be fair to your spouse.
Be humble to your spouse.
Make your home a paradise.
Be dedicated and energetic.
Be loyal to your relationship.
Be always a man or a woman.
Put music into your marriage.
Be always there for him or her.
Be valuable in the relationship.
Go into it prepared to work at it.
Make a good choice of a partner.
Respect and protect your spouse.
Be honest, frank, and dependable.
Look for character but not beauty.
Always seek your spouse's interest.
Be always available for him or her.
Be wholly committed to the marriage.
Don't be selfish or rude to your spouse.
Help him or her correct his or her faults.
Don't lie or be dishonest to your spouse.
Resolve financial problems by budgeting.
Be a husband or a wife in the relationship.
Be a father or a mother in the relationship.
Don't marry for money, but marry for love.
Be late for anything, but not for him or her.
Don't let your business come before him or her.
Give a love that only God can give your partner.
Put into it a one hundred percent effort and energy.
When there is disagreement, resolve it before night.
Love your spouse with all your heart, mind and soul.
Use peaceful methods to resolve issue that may arise.
Share his or her failures as well as his or her successes.
Encourage your spouse to keep growing in mind and in the relationship.
Prevent the third person – friends, lawyers or courts – from your marriage.

By Pius Yao Ashiara

Chapter 4

FATHER IN THE HOME

What a father is and what he must be: A father is a lone man traveling with his children to reach the Land of Canaan. Father, as a sower of seeds! A father has several seeds that he will sow in his family of children, with a mother as the second sower. There are going to be a Seed of God, Seed of love, Seed of joy, Seed of education and training, Seed of money, Seed of hard work, Seed of enthusiasm, Seed of encouragement, Seed of hope, and a Seed of happiness.

A father is a leader and the commander of his family. His leadership determines the success of his family. He lets his family follow him in his undertakings and does not say to them "Let us go!" but leads the way by guiding and counseling them with his experience.

God's words to the father: "Whatsoever a man soweth, that shall he also reap." — Galatians 6:7 (KJV). A father must be an architect of the family. His drawing will determine what kind of home his family will live in. The goal of a father is to be a good farmer. He does not want his seeds to be scattered on the ground and walked over by predators, nor some to fall on stones and eaten by birds. He does not want prodigal sons. He wants them to turn into "Mustard Seeds."

God created the Garden of Eden (which is our earth) and He made man and supported him with a woman. Man on that day of creation was endowed with qualities that made him a father. In addition, God made woman a mother who would help multiply the children of the earth.

It is easier having a mother in the home as the best companion on earth than any other person. A mother in the home is an angel, and if we treat her well, she won't mind giving her wings to us to fly.

Father/Mother Relationship: Father/Mother relationship must take the course of two travelers on a journey with a purpose to reach a destination both have planned. Their aim and vision must be one taken by guiding each other and making each other happy as they travel along. Their frequent stops on their journey should be for resting, stimulating and reflecting on their lives and the lives of their children.

Father/Son Relationship: Father/son relationship must take the form of two loving brothers as well as two loving friends who do everything together because together each one of them achieves more and seeks happiness, which they all share. Father and son are brothers, are cousins, are uncles, are companions, are friends, and are confidants. They must have a clean enduring relationship with each other, each one looking out for the other.

Father/daughter relationship: Father/daughter relationship must take the form of a loving brother and sister, and must be a boyfriend and a girlfriend who share their meals together, share their secrets together, and seek each other's welfare together. They must look out for each other. They must have an "open door approach" to each other in time of need and want.

Father/Mother-in-law Relationship: For one to maintain a cordial relationship with in-laws, one must try to ignore many things that will come in your relations. One cannot be inward-looking in matters but talk over amicably any disagreements that will affect the relationship. In-laws are older and are set in their ways and will want things done their way (which may be wrong). We must accept them but make our decisions the way we see fit.

Mother/Father-in-law Relationship: Problems may arise where the opinion of the father-in-law may be enlisted to help resolve an issue. This should be done discreetly and with respect to his opinion, considering his age and wisdom. In many cases a mother and father should try to find their own solution to their problem and assert their own decision.

Father/Friends: Maintain good relationship with your friends. When they visit your home, give them the warmest reception. But keep your married life to you and your wife only. Your wife must do the same with her friends. If there is a gift, offer it on their way out. Encourage your children to maintain a good relationship with their children as well.

Father's Day: what it means to children. They look on that day as a day of compliments for a job well done. They like to come around with flowers, food, cakes, and love to say: "Thank You" for being a great dad.

Another important factor in raising children is their religious life which is paramount to their growth and cannot be neglected. When religious belief gets into them, it prevents any wayward life. A father is god on earth who is endowed with all the tools one needs to raise good children.

A house is a home if there is a father.

— *Pius Yao Ashiara*

No father can live a great life without being a great father. As he grows into retirement, his children become his foundation that is made of steel instead of mortar and cement blocks from which he built his own marriage.

A father must be looking into the lives of his children as if they were pages of book he was looking through to find mistakes to correct. If a father has a son, he must remember that he is raising a child who will become a husband and someday may become a father. If he ever has children, he must become a responsible father.

When a man becomes a father, he should know that he is no longer a boy. Now all eyes of the world are upon him and demanding the best of him.

BE A GREAT FATHER THE WORLD WANTS

Chapter 5

MOTHER IS THE HOME

When God made the Garden of Eden He found that man will be lonely without a companion. Thus He made a woman as an aide to him.

Mother/Father Relationship: A mother and father must be a pupil and a teacher. The mother teaching the father all about a woman and motherhood and the father teaching the mother all about a man and fatherhood — from cooking to personal appearance — and pointing the way that makes for his intellectual growth as a man.

Mother/Daughter Relationship: Mother/Daughter relationship must take the form of two loving sisters as well as two loving friends who become to two beauticians that build a salon together, dress each other's hair, eat together, share sweaters and winter coats together, who do all things together because together each one of them achieves more and builds a stronger love for the other.

Mother/Son Relationship: Mother/son relationship must take the form of loving mother and father, loving brother and sister, and a boyfriend and a girlfriend who share their meals together, share their secrets together, and seek each other's welfare together, being there for each other. The goal of the mother is training the son in all that a woman may desire in a man.

Mother/Mother-in-law Relationship: For one to maintain a cordial relationship with in-laws, one must try to ignore many things that will come up in your relations.

Mother/Father-in-law Relationship: Problems may arise where the opinion of the father-in-law may be enlisted to help resolve an issue. This should be done discreetly and with respect to his opinion, considering his age and wisdom.

Mother/Friends: Maintain good relationships with your friends. When they visit your home, give them the warmest reception.

On each Mother's Day, we try to make your day a special one and like to express our appreciation for your care and offering yourself and filling all our needs.

A mother wants her home nice and neat, with her daily needs and wants available at all times. Her tapestries, drapes, blinds, and carpets are nice and clean. Her bed is well-dressed (and the most comfortable bed to sleep on) and that of the children. Her living room is welcoming and the appearance appealing to guests and visitors. Her kitchen must be in order and the best meals coming thereof. She makes sure all the food in the refrigerator is well labeled and dated.

A child is a mother's greatest asset and treasury. The food he eats, the clothes he wears, the place he sleeps, and the school he attends are very important to her, and she will not rest until these needs are satisfied.

Safety in the Home: A mother in the home must be detail-oriented and a watchdog checking daily on the heat and water system of the home that they run efficiently. *If the home has knives and guns and tools that hurt or destroy, they must be kept under lock and key and their use open only to those allowed to use them.*

If a mother has a daughter, she must remember that she is raising a child who will become a wife and someday may become a responsible mother. A mother must remember that at times some men consider women superfluous — some take advantage of a woman by leaving her for another woman after they had children; he assumes that if each man marries thirty women, there will still be remainders who will be looking for a good man to marry.

BE A GREAT MOTHER THAT THE WORLD WANTS

Chapter 6

CHILDREN IN THE HOME

Children are the future of the world. Once a child is born into a family, the first car is brought into the family, and we must create a driving lesson to train him.

Home is the first classroom of children, and here they are raised as sons and daughters who will become men and women and, perhaps, fathers and mothers of the future. They must be trained well before they enter the street. When neglected, we face a big danger in the future if they grow beyond the teen years.

Before they come out of the womb, we must start teaching them, and when they come into the world, we must teach them love of one another. When a child is born, his mind is an empty container which needs to be filled only with good things only. The first thing to put into his container is the love of God and respect and love for his fellow human beings. Always pound into his mind that without God he will have no great life and his life may be filled with worries, tragedies, and perhaps violence.

Before placing the newborn into the crib, we must immediately create an environment that will allow his mental expansion and mind growth. We must begin to train his eyes to beauty and provide his surroundings with only beauty. His ear must be trained to good listening and sound with songs, music, recitations and poems, and good speeches.

At home we must train him with prayers, cheerfulness, good smiles, and laughter and let him share only the joy of the home. Good manners, the power of personality, love, cheerfulness, smiles, laughter, and enthusiasm are the primary essentials of our lives, but they are never taught in the classroom; these have to be taught by parents before children leave their homes. Home is happiness; after that there is no place like home.

Anger, hate, jealousy, disappointments, and regret all begin early in a person's life, but they can be prevented early with love in the home by both parents giving love to each other. Make love their next meal, which should be the only thing anyone should know.

Divorce in Marriage: Divorce is evil. It destroys a wife and husband, making them enemies with a lifetime hatred for each other. It kills the human spirit, especially when a relationship is severed under this condition. When it comes, it plays a child against a father or a mother and promotes evil tendencies in children, or better yet it places children between a hard place and a rock. When it occurs, it makes a mother's life more difficult, which forces her to be in both places — a father and a mother place.

The attendant problem divorce brings into married people's life is many times violence or murder. We must seek harmony when children are involved in the marriage to avoid stress to the family. When it happens, attention does not get to the children, because a child becomes a basketball tossed between the divorced parents.

It is essential that parents and children have monthly conferences with each other to sort out matters, so that they stay away from divorce and everyone's ideas and opinion are respected.

Care around Children: Care around children is very important because their quick movement, in many cases, results in accidents, tragedies, or death. *A case in point:* A mother had only one son. They came from church, and when they got home, the mother, instead of parking her car and turning the engine off, held onto the brake while the engine was running.

She asked the son to go and open the garage door. While the kid was opening the door, her foot went off the brake pedal and the car drove into the child and the garage door, killing her son.

Everywhere, at every moment when the family is using a car or machine, it should be shut down and the kids seated in a car or before using a machine. What a tragedy that ended a promising young life!

A FATHER AND MOTHER OWE THE WORLD A GREAT CHILD

Chapter 7

THE HUMAN MIND

Train your brain and you have grain to feed you.

—*Pius Yao Ashiara*

Right this minute, walk to a mirror and take a look at yourself. You will observe the head resting on top of your entire body. It is the first part to see before the rest. And here lies your existence in life the human head.

God has given us a great machine to use all our lives. Everything we must have to live will be performed by this efficient but delicate equipment, the brain. The head has to be handled as a baby. It cannot be turned into a carriage or used in place of a horse or abused. As a baby in a crib, it must be well dressed and kept comfortable, provided with good pillows to sleep on. The force of the brain cannot be underestimated. Look about you! Medicine, skyscrapers, cars, jets, airplanes, trains, ships, and so on all came through the human brain. To set our brain aside and seek wealth of any kind outside this realm is waste of a lifetime. The brain is the center of the universe. A man or woman who depends chiefly on his or her own brain is more likely to achieve greater results than any other person. Our brains are given to us to keep them at work and to help us solve our problems in life. The person who does not recognize this fact falls short of his living.

The Human Mind is a demigod, but it has to be developed to think. At birth, the head, generally, appears first before the rest of the human body arrives. With a person standing, it is the first of the body resting on the neck and the rest of the body holding its head. From this conclusion we cannot argue that the head is the most important part of the human body. Within it is a vessel containing the human brain, and here resides the powerful human mind that makes us live as human beings. *A growing mind grows along with more advancing minds.* The mind, eyes, ears, mouth and our hands are relatives, and what each tells the mind is what the mind accepts.

The miracle of the mind: Anyone who has traveled by the airplane and arrived safely in another country or on another land should absolutely count on the power and force of the mind and respect everything that comes from it.

At birth it is empty and must be filled with knowledge through learning by the growing years. The early environment that is created for it determines its power and its efficacy. Each mind is a container. Many are poor. Some are mediocre. Some are well-developed. Few are rich. The mind is a machine; that is why we build machines. Let us take car steering to explain the workings of the mind. To drive a car, we have a manual for it so that we will not use it without care. A good care of all parts of the human being must be in harmony to give strength to it to operate.

The mind is a noiseless machine that ought to operate efficiently. Rest and sleep are its oil that keeps it running efficiently. It comes in horse power and delivers power in the same capacity. Those with great minds are those who come with the greatest ideas. Thomas Edison, Henry Ford, Benjamin Franklin, Ralph Waldo Emerson, Shakespeare, Plato, Disraeli, Bill Gates, and Steve Jobs are typical examples of great minds.

Steps for the mind: The mind develops like a staircase and grows in steps, depending on how much work is given to it. The more we train it, the stronger and more powerful it becomes. The group in which you live and work is very important to your "mind growth." The environment in which you were born, live, work, and learn has a significant part in your mind development.

Other people's minds can become a mirror for us to see through and learn from. Edison's electric bulb can become a magnificent tool for the development of another type of light-bulb.

Once something is invented, a door is opened for another mind to enter to discover something. The typewriter was invented, and a door was opened for computer to be invented. Once the PC was invented, a door was opened for Bill Gates' mind to develop software: Microsoft. Once the PC was invented, a door was opened for Steve Jobs' mind to build Apple II, Macintosh, iMac, iPod, iPhone, and iPad. Each one was plugged from the socket of Steve Jobs' work. The mind is an electric extension cord for other minds to plug into to draw power for new invention. The Internet opened the door for Mr. Zuckerberg to build facebook. The mind will always be leading us forward to develop and invent.

Building "Mental Cargoes" on the mind: A ship was traveling to South America and was overloaded with cargo. It was feared that if its weight was not reduced, there was danger the ship would drown in the course of the travel. The weight was reduced and the ship was able to travel without difficulty. This is the way humans load the mind, without concern about its weight, which develops into what I call "Mental Cargoes."

What impedes the mind from growth and working efficiently is the "mental cargoes" we put on our minds, one piled on top of another. Many of us put health mental cargoes, money mental cargoes, marital mental cargoes, divorce mental cargoes, mother-in-law mental cargoes, children mental cargoes, and maybe sorrow mental cargoes on our minds. Mental cargoes are barriers or mind bunglers. These weigh down our progress and our performance. If men and women can avoid loading the mind with negative mental cargoes and fill them with positive mental cargoes, they will work more efficiently and live longer. Keeping these mental cargoes on the mind without unloading them, holds back the mind from moving forward to whatever we plan. When we occupy the mind with mental cargoes, we have no empty places for new ideas to flow in, because it is packed full of negative loads.

Training the mind for peace and harmony: Peace and harmony make life run on a smooth road. Peace induces the mind and keeps it from agitation and lets it take its own course. It avoids intensity and force to obtain its result in a natural way. The moment we throw any violence on the mind, we create a chaos. The moment directs the mind to the achievement of that goal.

Building a foundation for the Mind: When a home has to be built, a more important attention should be paid to the foundation. The best materials selected by the builder's mind will determine the life of the building and so must we do for the mind. Before a building contractor builds a home, he seeks the materials necessary to give his home a strong foundation that will last through the years; so must we seek the right materials that will build a strong foundation of the mind. This has to be done before the teen years are over. If it is not done immediately when a person is born, it will be too difficult to give the proper strength to the mind.

The mind and life Problems: Sometimes culture is embedded in us so deeply that we cannot discover our minds nor see ourselves. At times problems are like a lion, a tiger, or a dog. When you approach them, they bark and snarl in your face. Unless you walk courageously to them, you cannot overcome them. In solving them, at times, it must turn into a fight that needs to be fought back. *The objective of a problem is to fight and wrestle with it.* We must look at the changing world to change our thinking and our way of life. To solve problems, think and look beyond your ordinary existence. Solving problems, measure the size of the problem to the size of the ocean. You will see how small your problem is, and it won't be difficult for you to solve.

When you see a human being walking with a head, there is some kind of mind inside him; respect that person because you do not know what is inside him. Like a tree, your mind expects you to stand alone. Leaning against other people is a temporary wall – it cannot keep you standing firm, because you are not standing alone as a tree does. Let your mind, goal, and work occupy you the way words occupied Ralph Waldo Emerson, Longfellow, Whitman, Frost, and Shakespeare. Like the way invention occupied Thomas Alva Edison. Like the way car-building occupied Henry Ford. Like the way iMac, iPod, iPhone, and so on occupied Bill Gates and Steve Jobs. The purpose of the mind is occupation. It is an efficient machine that must be working when not asleep.

Now, let us visit "Thinking." Let us make an experiment. Go into your bedroom. When you entered you saw that it was dark. What did you do? You groped through the darkness to find the electrical switch. (This means that you have been living in darkness before.) The switch you flipped changed your entire world and outlook and perception. It has brought you to see everything in front of you. It has brought you awakening and stimulation of the mind. You have driven away darkness and have developed thinking by the switch. The switch now becomes your "thinking tool" to let your mind not be subdued by inferior things. It has brought light to your whole self and your whole world.

Figure 1: Light Switch
is for thinking.

Mr. Thomas Edison spent many years to discover the electric light bulb. He drove away ignorance and darkness by a switch of electric light to tell us that our minds are gods and we should depend on them for our living. He who will pass the "light switch" and will be searching for a "thinking tool" elsewhere is less of a human being. The electrical switch is saying, "Open your eyes to see and think; it is a new day and a new world." The light switch you flip is a command for you to see and think, and it is telling you that gone are the days when Edison did not discover the light-bulb and we were living in darkness – superstition is gone, inferior mind is gone, mediocrity is gone, and there should be less ignorance. Submitting the mind to little things is gone. This tells us that we can now see and think better and more and can develop powerful minds. So the light switch is more a command to "think." The light switch is to think through darkness, through ignorance and primitivity. It is an eye opener for one to look more and think beyond his skull and environment to bring a change if he wants to be progressive. Airplanes, trains, cars, ships, computers, and cell phones are all thinking tools around us to think more and to think better. *The light switch is an instructor to mankind.*

Concentration: The mind is a car with a steering wheel and requires concentration while driving it. It requires a straight course and focus.

Like neat and clean clothes to the body, the mind must also seek neatness and cleanliness to stay working efficiently. It has to be emptied from time to time of impurities to create room for new ideas. Its thinking of today should be an improvement on yesterday's ideas. Its ideas today should be a changed and improved work for tomorrow.

Mental Rest Stops: Like rest stops on the highway, where after a long drive we give rest to our bodies and the car, we must give the mind mental rest as well to rejuvenate us in our thinking. This will bring relaxation to the mind from time to time. It will more or less make us new persons, which will increase our productive ability at tasks given to the mind.

Chapter 8

REVERENCE FOR THE ALMIGHTY DOLLAR

Figure: 1: *I, Kevin Agbeko Ashiara, hold these currencies on behalf of Almighty Everlasting God who designated me for this order that long illness or death to those who would adulterate the dollar through counterfeiting, drugs, drug trafficking, murder, sex, illegal manipulation, bribery, greed, kickbacks or any false means of making and spending it in spirit shall face long sickness or death. The dollar is once again consecrated in His name:* **"IN GOD WE TRUST."** *It shall be the most powerful currency in the world. Kevin Agbeko Ashiara was born in Elizabeth General Hospital in New Jersey on June 10, 1993. A year after his birth he never spoke, and doctors found out that he was autistic but concluded in his case, he would never talk and does not talk. Teaching him brought the idea to open a school for his disability,* **"School for the Development of GreatMIND"** *to teach Life's Guidance: Life from Birth to Death. This school is in the works. The interpretation of the gown colors: Black — life is serious business, therefore we must take it with seriousness; Red — is blood (to live one must sweat through his blood by work alone to earn his living); Gold — are the arms and hands that signifies wealth and he who uses them efficiently will be wealthy; Green — stands for peace among people throughout the world and the mind must be a peaceful place to conquer the world. The Hat is the human brain where the mind delivers everything we need to live in life.*

God has prepared man for living by giving him a Mind, Eyes, Ears, Mouth and Hands with years to live, and under all these came a package called "Life."

The above dollar bill is next to God. Once God's name is written on it, it has the power of God within and cannot be adulterated. Faith, courage, fearlessness, trust, honesty, loyalty and hope are within, and it has to be worshipped through prayer and respect.

Practically speaking, the dollar bill is God that passes through our hands every second we spend it. It ought to be held by a clean hand. Once

Figure 2: "IN GOD WE TRUST"

we have God written on it, it is authentic and cannot be accumulated or used in any other way than through sweat, thinking, use of muscle, physical labor, hard work, and receiving it in a *genuine way*. If it is used or accepted through drugs, murder, sex, or political favors or offers, kickbacks, bribery and so on, one is guilty of a cardinal sin, and God will never forgive the user. Punishment comes with of loss of career, position, shame, long illness, sickness, suicide, murder, or death that we do not physically see because the dollar bill has a powerful spirit behind it. The dollar bill is God passing through every hand, and it is backed by a strong spirit. *The dollar currency is a holy tool for transactions.* Money is the most powerful tool in the world. When it touches love, it brings happiness. When it touches hunger, it brings satiety. When it touches anger, it brings separation, murder, or death.

The faith in the Dollar Currency: Kevin Agbeko Ashiara has brought a message to the world. Everyone must listen and obey God's orders. Our economy, the United States of America's economy, is built on "**IN GOD WE TRUST.**" This is the concrete foundation of the United States of America. [January 1 to January 7 every year will be observed as the week for Reverence for the Almighty Dollar, and it shall be observed and complied so.] All banks and financial institutions must now erect the one-dollar-bill flag on its premises just like the national flag in permanent reverence for the dollar.

Gospel of Conscience: Conscience is a god that sits in judgment on our thoughts and actions. It is the moral monitor that asks the question, "What I am about to do with my money, will it be right or wrong?" The person with a good conscience is one who does things though no one sees him. He is the person who obeys the laws behind the public eye. He may hold the national flag on Independence Day, Memorial Day, Veteran's Day, Labor Day, Mothers' Day, Father's Day, and Valentine Day, but he is discounted among good citizens if he does not live and work by his conscience and seek the welfare of his fellow citizens and country; he or she is less of a human being. To be a good citizen and nation lover, everyone must first be a teacher through character and good conduct. He must have a heart and mind of a soldier, fireman, police officer or a defender of his nation.

When we discovered our son's disability, at first we were disappointed because no human being expects a wrong thing, but we looked over the whole thing as a gift from God to study before we can appreciate him. However, we tried to find out through prayers to God what kind of gift is he to us. Our older son and second daughter also came with the same questioning. Our conclusion was that he is a gift to mankind to correct the wrongs. When we realized this, I set up a classroom at home, teaching him, to find out the hidden secret in this young man. I have been doing an extensive research about his whole being. Since he is nonverbal, he talks to me through dreams and the use of the microphone by tapping his lips, and I in turn tap my lips with the microphone, and this action sets me talking naturally for him.

Investigation: Upon my first investigation I found out that the human being is the universe wrapped in a small package. And if my family continues to seek the answer, we will find the solution and understanding.

We decided to take this package apart and examine what it contains. At the age of ten he developed his own organizational skill and his own personal rules.

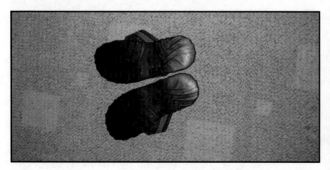 

Figure 3: Kevin Agbeko Ashiara's bathroom slippers.

From time to time he would arrange his bathroom slippers in exact position, measuring against the right foot or left foot ⁻ the right foot slipped backward ⁻ and brought to you. If you tried to change them to the right way, he would refuse but arranged them the way he wanted.

Using Talking Words: Since he does not talk, I read this poem to him every time before we start classes:

Think and think! Think and think!
Before you do anything: Think!
Everybody must think to do!
Think critically! Think hard! Think fast!
Reach the depth of your mind to think.
Stimulate the mind to think.
Reflect the mind to think.
Thinking is the clock on the mind.
Say it! Spell it! Sing it!

— Pius Yao Ashiara

I suspended teaching him the alphabets and concentrated on words that would stimulate his mind, e.g., think, head, mind, speak, talk, sing, or try to make him say something.

Figure 4: God; Think; Thank. Think God; Thank God.

The first three words I used in teaching him were **"God," "Think,"** and **"Thank"** (**Think God; Thank God**). We do this every morning and every evening. I try to reach his mind by presenting these picture words before his eyes and turned them into his next meal. Alongside I use the plastic alphabets teaching him colors — red, yellow, green, blue, purple, etc.:

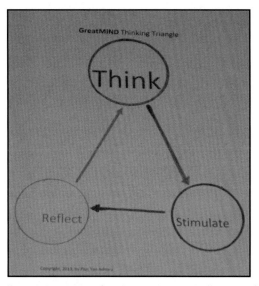

Figure 5*: I call this* **"GreatMIND Thinking Triangle."** *It is the concrete foundation* (**ConcreteMIND***) to the mind before the alphabets. In using the word* **"God,"** *I raise my right hand into the sky;* **"Think,"** *I let him tap his forehead with his figure while repeating the word and*

I do the same. In using the word **"Thank,"** *I give him a handshake. In using the word* **"stimulate,"** *I use two coffee cups with hot chocolate (his favorite) from left and right hands, then swapping the liquid into one another. In using the word* **"reflect,"** *I take him into my research laboratory before a picture of the ocean and turn it on vibration, and we stare at the movement of the ocean constantly in silence. We never worried about the alphabets. We work with these words to get them conditioned to his mind. Before we go to school, the mind has to be trained first and the first training we should receive is to practice with the "GreatMIND Thinking Triangle" and condition it to the mind as the alphabets. This will become the foundation and powerhouse of the mind.*

The Mind has to be nourished and trained early from the womb. We will only achieve this through the use of **"GreatMIND** Thinking" Concrete Construction Foundation (**ConcreteMIND**).

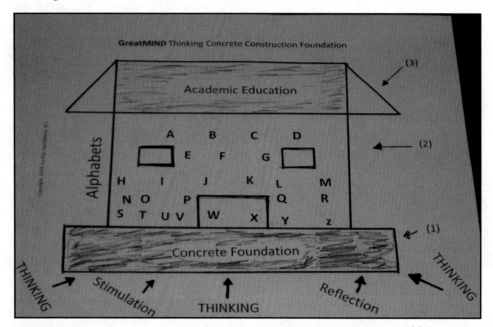

Figure 6: *This picture shows the development of the mind like a home starting from (1)* **GreatMIND** *Thinking Concrete Construction Foundation (***ConcreteMIND***), (2) The Walls, and (3) The Roof. Shown are* **"thinking,"** **"stimulation,"** *and* **"reflection."** *The* **GreatMIND** *Thinking Concrete Construction Foundation (***ConcreteMIND***) should be trained before the alphabets and the alphabets before academic education. The* **GreatMIND** *Thinking Concrete Construction Foundation should be the First Floor of Education.*

"**GreatMIND** Thinking" Concrete Construction Foundation (**ConcreteMIND**) is where thinking, stimulation, and reflection must start before the alphabets. The alphabets are a subject of study. The mind must be trained to practice **"thinking," "stimulation,"** and **"reflection"** the moment a person is born. If the **GreatMIND** Thinking Concrete Construction Foundation (**ConcreteMIND**) is not strong, it cannot hold the walls and roof in place. The mind left alone without training will become a hat in the wind blown here and there.

After the worship of God, the next thing human beings worship is money. It is what the whole world worships as the medium of exchange for love, goods and services. The faith held in it by men and women is the strongest in every life. *If husband and wife would hold the same faith in their relationship as the faith held in money, marriages would not fail.*

Financial Institutions: Any person, bank, or financial institution that indulges in fraud, false money, or manipulates the dollar in the wrong way — its managers and manipulators will suffer *long sickness or death.*

Warning: The moment you allow someone to persuade you in the wrong use of money, know that the person is of a "little mind an inferior person." On the other hand, anyone who invites you through thinking and work to realize money, that person is of a "**GreatMIND.**"

The **School for the Development of GreatMIND** *Lecture Platform:*

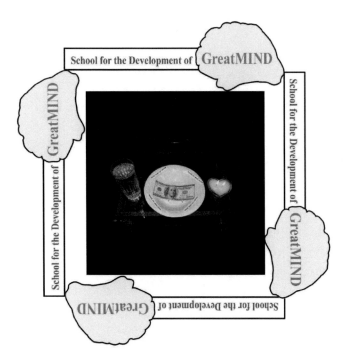

Figure 7: *This is **GreatMIND** Lecture Platform. When dropped on the floor of a room or on the ground in the open air, it represents a classroom. When Kevin Agbeko Ashiara is standing on it, it means lesson or lecture is going on.*

The **School for the Development of GreatMIND** is an outdoor and indoor and online school for *Life's Guidance: From Birth to Death*. Classes will be held anywhere in the open air. When the **GreatMIND** Lecture Platform is dropped on the floor in a room or on the ground in the open air, anywhere, the place becomes automatically a classroom. It will promote annually one week nation reading among children and adults.

This is the message Kevin Agbeko Ashiara is bringing from God to the world.

Chapter 9

THE PERCEPTION OF LIFE AND AMERICA

The corridor of life is a roadmap for the way to live that will take us on a mission beyond rising and sleeping. It will make us reflect upon life that is before us before it begins. We are entering a world — the earth — a world we have never seen before, but a world with promise we hope to be good, safe, and happy, the ultimate goal of LIFE. *The corridor of life is Life's Guidance: From Birth to Death.*

Most importantly, life is problem solving. It is a puzzle that comes with struggles, sorrows, tragedies, sadness, unhappiness, misfortunes, misery, murder, you name it. Life will come with problems that we cannot avoid. We are made to take them and find solutions for them that will make our lives true life.

This is your life's Google, MapQuest, and GPS. It is to guide you in life's travel and journey. Obey it just as a driver will follow instructions from Google, MapQuest, and GPS. We must study the lives of our statesmen. We have seen and heard of many lives and read many books written before us. These are books filled with struggles, pain, suffering, wailing, groaning, weeping, crying, sorrowing, and urging us to look at lives and see what led to their agonies. Take Abraham Lincoln, Benjamin Franklin, John F. Kennedy, Frederick Douglass, Booker T. Washington, Martin Luther King, Jr. Some are telling and reminding us how to lead great lives. They are telling that suffering is reduced, and no one has to walk 50 miles to borrow books. In our midst are schools, colleges, and libraries. In America, for every five blocks there is a school of some kind. These are at the fingertips for everyone to enjoy and work for.

The foreigner in the United States of America: When you take an airplane and it is able to bring you over the ocean to another land, you face a challenge to be a *thinker and an honest person.* This shows you the miracle of the human mind and that is where you should reach for living. When you enter the United States of America, you enter freedom. You may have had political issues against you in your home country and want a safe haven. This tells you that America has a kind heart and should be respected. Please do not disrespect the United States of America because it is God's nation and any wrong done to her gets punished.

You may have come with a student's visa to get an education, and this should be your primary aim. Do not form gangs to murder or defraud us or what will make some of us lose our name. A name is the only thing that belongs to everyone and if you must make someone born in his own country to change his name, you may be considered a murderer. How would you like to think your wrongdoing will affect the country you came from? What will be the chance for those of your people with genuine hearts and minds that really need to educate themselves and go back? How would you feel if an American citizen would not want to deal with your kind?

If you would live in America for a while, you are an "American," though you do not have documents that represent it, because you will be enjoying American food and the labor of America to build your own life; that is why in your heart and mind you must respect and protect America. Many people who are hard hit by poverty in their country turn to material possessions instead of education to make a better life than they had in their home country; they turn to fraud, quick money schemes to destroy America whose good name has brought them to this land of opportunity. Every crime or sin has a transcript. It will print someday. Every "good or wrong" done in life is a seed we plant; given time, it will germinate and sprout, and all eyes will see it.

In your country you may be only a drop of water, but when you come to the United States of America, you can expand into a river moving forward, maybe even a lake to build a dam, or you can become the ocean with the force of the tide to accommodate boats and ships. Or you can become an eagle and own the sky.

Recognition of Women: A wife is the right hand of a husband. She makes many decisions behind the scenes we do not know about when her husband is in authority. When a monument is built for a statesman or an important figure in society, a monument of the wife must be built next to his to recognize marriage and to proclaim it as a union of two people until death. Let us say when President Bill Clinton dies and we must build a monument for him, his wife Hilary Clinton must also receive a monument.

What America does for its citizens: American Government knows that if she does not have social security for its workers and deducts against unemployment, disability, and retirement, many of its workers who lose their jobs will not even have a bus fare to get home. People in the rank-and-file will be severely punished. Social Security, good job! You are an ornament on our society.

Success is a construction road that is never finished.

—*Pius Yao Ashiara*

Where do you want your name to be after you are gone through this world? Will it be among the Popes? Will you be among the presidents of the world? Will you be among the Secretary-Generals of the United Nations? Will you be among the Supreme Court Judges? Or will your name be behind the great walls of the world? Named after streets or monuments or statutes erected for you? Or do you want the history of your passing through to say you were a drunk? Or a criminal? Or simply you were a loser? Decide on what to tell the world you want to be.

ABOUT THE AUTHOR

After studying at home, Mr. Pius Yao Ashiara entered Stenotype Academy and graduated in 1976 with a 97% class rank. He took courses in Desktop Publishing and Computer Repairs at the Essex County Vocational Schools. He continued his education at Brooklyn College and through Project Deep at Essex County College and graduated in Business Administration. He further studied Business Management at Rutger's University, Newark, New Jersey. Mr. Ashiara had worked as a Production Executive in the publishing industry for the past 28 years – a field he loves and associates with great minds that he has turned into the **School for the Development of GreatMIND**. This school he is developing will eventually be launched based on a work he has been researching on his autistic son for the past twenty years.

He has worked in various capacities for 28 companies – from Singer Sewing Machine Company as a Porter to Burger King as a Crew Chief – in New York and New Jersey. Mr. Ashiara runs the **School for the Development of GreatMIND** from his basement, where he trains infants and children in their homes in the art of seeing by the eyes and hearing by the ear and by the art of listening. He has developed his own course in *Life's Guidance: From Birth to Death* — where he continues to research into "human life" and his autistic child. He is an avid reader and an independent scholar. His goal is to promote thinking, education, reading and enthusiasm in the individual.